School Improvement:

An Unofficial Approach

Improving Schools Series
Series Editors: Alma Harris and Jane McGregor

How to Improve your School – Jean Rudduck and Julia Flutter

Improving Schools in Difficulty – edited by Paul Clarke

Improving Schools in Exceptionally Challenging Circumstances – Alma Harris, Judith Gunraj, Sue James, Paul Clarke and Belinda Harris

Improving Schools through Collaborative Enquiry – edited by Hilary Street and Julie Temperley

Improving Schools through External Intervention – Chris Chapman

Leading Teachers – Helen M. Gunter

School Improvement:
An Unofficial Approach

Martin Thrupp

continuum
LONDON • NEW YORK

Continuum International Publishing Group
The Tower Building   15 East 26th Street
11 York Road   New York
London SE1 7NX   NY 10010

British Library Cataloguing-in-Publication Data
A catalogue record for this book is available from the British Library.

ISBN: 0–8264–6503–X (hardback)
        0–8264–6504–8 (paperback)

Library of Congress Cataloging-in-Publication Data
A catalog record for this book is available from the Library of Congress.

Typeset by Fakenham Photosetting Limited, Fakenham, Norfolk
Printed and bound in Great Britain by MPG Books Ltd., Bodmin, Cornwall

Contents

Acknowledgements	ix
Abbreviations and acronyms	xi
Series Editors' Foreword	xiii
1 Introduction	1
2 Always winter and never Christmas	9
3 Just one piece of Turkish Delight?	29
4 Even the trees are on her side	51
5 Best keep down here	79
6 A strange, sweet noise	105
Recommended reading	117
Notes	121
References	125
Index	140

For Grace and Simon

Acknowledgements

I would like to thank colleagues who have contributed to this book in one way or another including Noeline Alcorn, Stephen Ball, Mike Bottery, Carol Campbell, Marianne Coleman, Nesta Devine, Peter Earley, Jennifer Evans, Deborah Fraser, David Gillborn, Richard Hatcher, Hugh Lauder, Ruth Lupton, Mark Olssen, Richard Smith, Pat Thompson, Carol Vincent, Philip Woods, Nigel Wright and Terry Wrigley. Although I have benefited greatly from our various conversations, responsibility for the text remains mine. I have also gained numerous insights from the teachers and heads in my graduate classes at King's College London and the Institute of Education, University of London over the last five years: in this case too many people to mention but you have challenged and inspired. It is important to mention Alma Harris and Jane McGregor, Series Editors, and Christina Parkinson and Alexandra Webster of Continuum who have all been very patient and supportive. Finally, I am very grateful to Ceri Brown for proofreading the final draft.

Abbreviations and acronyms

ATL	Association of Teachers and Lecturers
BECTA	British Educational Communications and Technology Agency
BERA	British Educational Research Association
CASE	Campaign for State Education
CEN	Communities Empowerment Network
CSBM	Certificate of School Business Management
DfES	Department for Education and Skills
EAZ	Education Action Zone
EiC	Excellence in Cities
EMAG	Ethnic Minority Achievement Grant
EMAL	Educational Management and Leadership
ESRC	Economic and Social Research Council
FSM	Free School Meals
GTC	General Teaching Council
HEADLAMP	Headteacher Leadership and Management Programme
HIP	Headteacher Induction Programme
HMC	Headmasters' & Headmistresses' Conference
HMI	Her Majesty's Inspectors of Schools
IRR	Institute of Race Relations
KS	Key Stage
LEA	Local Education Authority
LPSH	Leadership Programme for Serving Headteachers
NAHT	National Association of Headteachers
NASUWT	National Association of Schoolmasters Union of Women Teachers
NCLB	No Child Left Behind
NCSL	National College for School Leadership
NFER	National Foundation for Educational Research

NgfL	National grid for Learning
NLNS	National Literacy and Numeracy Strategies
NPEA	National Primary Education Alliance
NphA	National Primary Headteachers Association
NPQH	The National Professional Qualification for Headteachers
NUT	National Union of Teachers
Ofsted	Office for Standards in Education
OSI	Official School Improvement
PANDA	Performance and Assessment Report
PAT	Professional Association of Teachers
PLASC	Pupil Level Annual School Census
PRP	Performance-Related Pay
QCA	Qualifications and Curriculum Authority
SAT	Standardized Achievement Test
SEN	Special Educational Needs
SES	Socio-economic Status
SFCC	Schools Facing Challenging Circumstances
SHA	Secondary Heads Assocation
SRB	Single Regeneration Budget
TES	*Times Educational Supplement*
TTA	Teacher Training Agency

Series Editors' Foreword

Those reading this book will undoubtedly question why in this series we have included a text that not only calls into question the very idea of improving schools but also challenges the current policies and practice aimed at school improvement? Put simply, to respond, this book is a much needed alternative reference point for those in the school improvement field, where it could be argued that a particular orthodoxy has taken hold. This book will irritate, challenge and confront many academics, practitioners and policy-makers who have devoted much of their professional careers in the name of school improvement. It will certainly not be a book that is read and forgotten as its messages are too powerful and its critique too forensic.

The issues Martin Thrupp raises and the questions he asks are much needed in a policy context that remains wedded to standard-based reform as the main lever of school improvement. His critique of managerialism highlights the limitations of performativity to raise standards within our education system and other systems around the world. In the USA the 'No Child Left Behind' policy has largely failed to secure the impact expected or to raise performance in schools in the poorest districts. The drive to raise standards in difficult or challenging contexts has become a central and urgent issue in education policy on an international scale.

The punitive 'improvement' measures associated with 'No Child Left Behind' are not too distant from those currently identified by Thrupp as being central to 'official school improvement' (OSI). The labelling, targeting and reconstitution of 'failing schools in the USA', sometimes with private sector involvement, combines a high degree of accountability with myopia towards the social and economic problems that envelop these schools. This is not too dissimilar, Thrupp argues, from the 'official school improvement' approaches that prevail in England where those schools in the most disadvantaged areas are expected, through their own efforts, to overcome deep-rooted and long-term socio-economic problems and to produce better results.

It is no accident that schools labelled as underpeforming are disproportionately located in disadvantaged areas but it is a fact often conveniently ignored. As Andy Hargreaves (2004) suggests, there is an emergent 'apartheid of school improvement' where those schools who are performing well within the system are given greater latitude and freedom from external intrusion while those performing less well are under constant scrutiny and find themselves in receipt of continual external intervention. Thrupp suggests that OSI has seemed like Narnia's long winter 'impoverished, mean spirited and with dissidents frozen out by a range of discursive, contractual, performance management and inspection processes'.

In this book the dissidents' voice is heard very loudly. The challenges and claims made are hard hitting and unequivocal. Thrupp's critique of the National College for School Leadership is probably one of the first to be published in such a detailed and extensive form. Whatever one thinks of his analysis, he does make the point that since the NCSL was established, there have been but few dissenting voices brave enough to put their criticism into print. As Thrupp notes, with 50 per cent of funding for research into leadership coming from the NCSL, those in academic positions who need such funding may be forgiven for 'playing the game'. Some of those who have worked with the NCSL in a research capacity, which includes one of the series editors, have undoubtedly experienced a tension between the need to secure funding and the type of the research being commissioned.

While silence might be a necessity for those seeing research funding from the NCSL, the voices of writers such as Thrupp, Hatcher and Gunter have been heard and have raised questions about current conceptions of leadership. Their voices represent growing disquiet amongst the academic community at the proliferation of what Gronn has termed 'designer leadership' and the narrow conceptualization of leadership practice. In practice, this narrow conceptualization of leadership is currently being challenged and eroded away through initiatives like the NCSL's 'Network Learning Communities'. Interestingly, Thrupp has given little space to one of the most hopeful, ambitious and practitioner-focused developments that the NCSL has initiated, developed and supported. This powerful model of school transformation not only has teachers at its core but is premised upon networking, knowledge transfer and student voice. Its principles are those that endorse innovation, experimentation and collaboration. Its models of leadership are those that equate with learner-centred, instructionally focused and distributed leadership practice. Far from endorsing the OSI agenda, the 'Networking Learning Communities' represents the very antithesis of an instrumental and narrow means of improvement.

While there is much in this book to reflect upon, to like and to debate there is also much to disagree upon. Not all school improvement is of an official kind, and initiatives like the 'Networked Learning Communities' are presenting schools with an opportunity to create their own school improvement agendas through collaboration. Inevitably, this means that improvement approaches will be more locally sensitive and contextually specific which Thrupp agrees is long overdue in the field.

Whatever the limitations of the school improvement field, in its non-official form it has consistently worked with teachers, parents and students to generate alternative models of school development and change from those imposed or mandated. Some have succeeded, some have failed and some have simply chosen not to confront the underlying structural inequalities that have rendered schools in need of improvement in the first place. Some of the writing has been naïve and apologist, some of the models of improvement simplistic and under-theorized. This book by Martin Thrupp is important because it presents a wealth of careful critique. Interestingly there is little discussion of alternative approaches or ways forward.

What this book also offers is a way forward, albeit not of the kind generally proposed by school improvement researchers. Thrupp argues that teachers, heads and others involved in schools should actively contest New Labour's educational reforms, openly where feasible or more covertly where necessary. This is fighting talk, but Thrupp presents a range of anecdotal and research evidence to illustrate that there are many possibilities for action.

Significantly, Thrupp suggests it is not necessary to be a 'radical' or an 'activist' to want to contest damaging school reform. To what extent this 'unofficial' agenda will appeal to practitioners is uncertain. What is clear though is that this book offers an important challenge to education policy and school practice today.

Alma Harris and Jane McGregor
Series Editors

1 Introduction

One of the nice things about being a parent is that you get to relive some of the pleasures of childhood, at least vicariously. So it was that my children recently reintroduced me to the enchanting world of *The Lion, the Witch and the Wardrobe* by C.S. Lewis. For anyone unfamiliar with this book or its film versions, it is the story of four children who are evacuated from London because of the air raids during the Second World War. While playing in the big country house to which they have been sent, one of the children, Lucy, climbs into a wardrobe and finds a secret entrance into Narnia, a snowy land of pine forests. In Narnia it turns out that a White Witch has made herself Queen, put the land under the spell of permanent winter and imposed a reign of terror where the trees and animals are her spies and dissidents are turned to stone. Nevertheless when all the children later go through the wardrobe to Narnia, they meet animals who want to overthrow the White Witch. With a good many adventures and the coming of Aslan the Lion, the White Witch is duly dispensed with. By the end of the book spring has triumphed over winter, hope over despair, good over evil.

The religious, specifically Christian, imagery in *The Lion, the Witch and the Wardrobe* is hard to miss. At the same time, rereading this book made me think how often English schooling under New Labour's complex of education policies – nicely summed up by Hatcher (1998) as 'Official School Improvement' (OSI) – has seemed like Narnia's long winter: impoverished, mean-spirited and with dissidents frozen out by a range of discursive, contractual, performance management and inspection processes, if not actually turned to stone. There are other similarities too. Just as many of the living things in Narnia are in the service of the White Witch, it often seems that most of those in the education sector – teachers, headteachers, Local Education Authority staff, Ofsted inspectors, consultants and even some academics – want to work, or find it necessary to work, within the discourses of OSI rather than question them. Yet as in Narnia, perhaps not all is lost. There are teachers, heads, academics and others who are working in various ways to counter OSI and recent shifts in policy illustrate that although persistent it is not immutable.

Along the same lines *School Improvement: An Unofficial Approach* offers a critical response to the dominance of the OSI agenda. It uses some of the themes of C.S. Lewis's story to introduce discussion of the damaging nature of OSI, support for it amongst practitioners and academics, where OSI is being contested and the possibilities of undermining it further. Given OSI's often unjust and anti-educational nature, ways to challenge or subvert it need to be found and this book seeks to explore and encourage 'unofficial' school improvement responses among school practitioners and those who work with them: responses which can help to unsettle OSI, mitigate some of its worst effects, and perhaps help to eventually dislodge it.

A chapter outline

Chapter 2 'Always winter and never Christmas' provides a trenchant critique of OSI. OSI involves a market, managerial and performative approach to education which stems from a vision of individual and national economic competitiveness. It emphasizes testing, target setting, performance management and managerial school leadership. These are features of policy in many countries but they are particularly intense in England. While it is clear that most people, both in and out of the education sector, would agree there is *some* kind of problem with OSI, the nature and extent of their critiques differ markedly. This chapter highlights both immediate and more fundamental deficiencies.

A tempting argument against taking an unofficial approach to school improvement would be that OSI is changing over time to become more progressive. Chapter 3 'Just one piece of Turkish Delight?' takes this possibility seriously and explores it though analyses of two different areas of OSI policy. One is the Primary Strategy which in various ways seems to represent an opening up of the English primary school curriculum. The other is the Office for Standards in Education (Ofsted) which is seen by many to have changed for the better in recent years. Discussion of these two areas will show that while OSI is certainly evolving over time, to date there is no sign of it shifting so fundamentally that it need not be contested.

Chapter 4 'Even the trees are on her side' acts as a bridge between critique of OSI policy and discussion of how it can be contested by heads and teachers. I begin by considering the National College for School Leadership (NCSL) which, although a government agency, is often seen to be about addressing the professional concerns of headteachers and others in leadership positions in schools. The reality, as illustrated here by exploring its website, is that the NCSL is very much about promoting the OSI agenda. This chapter then goes on to examine a recent debate between writers who have argued that heads generally 'mediate' policy rather than comply with it and others who have argued that heads are thoroughly captured by OSI. I conclude that the argument for mediation is weak but that the debate will remain unresolved without better research into the day-to-day practices of heads. Finally some recent perspectives on teachers' responses to OSI are considered. As with the 'mediation' debate, these accounts are not really close enough to the work of teachers to draw firm conclusions. Nor do they address obvious forms of teacher contestation such as the work undertaken by unions and professional associations.

The question of contestation may be partly an empirical one, but Chapter 5, 'Best keep down here' illustrates that there is no shortage of ways contestation could be occurring. It begins by considering contestation at the national and regional level then moves along a spectrum towards more surreptitious ways for individual schools and their staff to contest OSI. Reflecting the chapter title, I argue that contestation practices will often have to be covert because of the culture of audit and surveillance within which schools now operate. There are many possibilities but as with other forms of contestation, hidden practices have both advantages and disadvantages.

A difficulty for heads and teachers wanting to contest OSI and recast school improvement as part of a much wider social and educational project has been the reactive, uncritical nature of much of the school improvement literature. My final chapter, 'A strange sweet noise' begins by noting how academic writers in this area have been underplaying the limitations of OSI to wittingly or unwittingly influence practitioners to go along with it and this chapter considers some likely explanations for this problem of 'textual apologism'. But updating my earlier discussion in *Education Management in Managerialist Times: Beyond the Textual Apologists* (Thrupp and Willmott 2003), this final chapter notes promising developments in some recent shifts to more contextualized school improvement analysis and the work of a 'dissenting' school improvement author (Wrigley 2003). These developments illustrate that although not yet common, there are alternative sources of textual inspiration for practitioners in the school improvement area. Wrigley's book *Schools of Hope* also acts as a reminder to educators not to reinvent the wheel when progressive thinking from previous decades can provide many leads.

A vocabulary for responding critically to OSI

One difficulty in writing about critical responses to OSI is to find a suitable vocabulary. A decade ago Woods (1995: 8–10) came up with five categories of primary teacher response to the introduction of the National Curriculum: 'resistance', 'appropriation', 'resourcing', 'enrichment' and 're-routing'. These followed Osborn and Broadfoot's (1992) categorization of teacher's options (apart from cooperating with reform) as 'resistance', 'incorporation' or 'retreatism'. The strength of these categories is that they were grounded in detailed research with teachers and gave a flavour of how they were reacting to policy. At the same time such categories pose a number of problems for thinking about how to respond to OSI today.

First, the notion of 'resistance' used as above is only being used to describe the most obvious kinds of resistant practices, yet most of the other responses raised by Woods and Osborn and Broadfoot can also be regarded as subtle forms of resistance. Indeed overt resistance to OSI is understandably rare given the punitive consequences for individuals and schools. The notion of resistance is also politically loaded because like 'subversive' and 'activist', it often carries the implication of taking up a self-consciously radical stance. In contrast I would argue that working against OSI should be regarded as a legitimate everyday activity for teachers and heads precisely because they are educators who should have the best interests of children at heart. Thus while Gale and Densmore (2003) propose a 'radical democratic agenda' for schooling and Sachs (2003) has written about *The Activist Teaching Profession,* many practitioners will be uncomfortable with such terms to describe their work. A point made by Indian writer Arundhati Roy is relevant here. She describes the term 'writer-activist' as no more eloquent than the term 'sofa-bed': 'It's a comment on the reduction of the meaning of being a writer you know. Why should it be that I have to be an "activist"?' (cited in Hare 2004). Likewise, *as educators*, all teachers and heads should be allowed a concern with fair and educational education policy – not just a 'resistant' few.

Second, concepts like 'appropriation' and 'incorporation' can be slippery if used to imply that if approached creatively enough, the policy framework – in our case, OSI – need not present any constraints to progressive practice in schools. A similar case of trying to have one's cake and eat it too is the argument, discussed in Chapter 4, that headteachers are 'mediating' policy: working within it towards more just and educational ends. Of course there is *some* truth in this: policy is never simply 'implemented' and practitioners never simply 'comply'. But 'mediation' should not be used as the primary organizing concept for responding critically to reform because there are powerful controls on the activities of schools and their staff under OSI which remove many possibilities of acting progressively while remaining within OSI. For instance, SATs testing, target setting or Ofsted inspections all have powerful effects on school cultures and on individual students. Depending on their approach, staff working within OSI might reduce the impact of these performative features but there is no way of 'mediating' them to the extent that they are no longer damaging.

Third, although helpful for thinking about different kinds of practitioner response to reform, the problem with such typologies as those developed by Woods (1995) and Osborn and Broadfoot (1992) is that they tend to essentialize and compartmentalize – here is an 'appropriator', there a 'resister' and so on. While Woods (1995: 10) does note that 'it may be that these are predominant modes in some schools and with some teachers ... [but] elsewhere, a combination might be experienced', in fact practitioners' stances and actions are likely to be very complicated, depending for instance on the issue being faced. For the purposes of this book it seems less important to categorize responses and more important to allow for their complexity.

For all of these reasons, in this book I have chosen to use the notion of 'contesting' OSI. Semantics perhaps, but for many in education circles 'contesting' OSI will sound a more productive and legitimate activity than 'resisting' it. 'Contesting' and contestation can be used as umbrella terms to avoid getting caught up in existing typologies of teachers' responses to reform or the need to develop new ones. In this book contestation is intended to include all practitioner activities which seek to respond critically to OSI. These include critique (or 'textual dissent') as well as the many public and more covert practices which can be taken to challenge, modify or subvert the effects of OSI, as discussed in Chapters 4 to 6.

Who this book has been written for

Although *School Improvement: An Unofficial Approach* focuses on OSI under New Labour and ways in which this can be contested by England's heads and teachers, it is also intended to be useful to people in other education sector roles in England such as LEA staff, union officials, governors, teacher educators and academics as well as having wider international relevance. To begin with, there is no assumption here that the task of contesting OSI is exclusive to heads and teachers, rather it is a challenge that anyone with a role in English schooling can take up, although contributions will obviously vary according to role. In particular it would be a mistake to assume that all those whose job it is to promote OSI are blind to its limitations. For instance, in a study undertaken with colleagues in the inner-London borough of Wyeham (Thrupp *et al.* 2003, Thrupp *et al.* 2004, as discussed in Chapter 2), we found people working at the LEA level who were charged with delivering OSI initiatives to schools but who were more critical of it than many of the heads and teachers we spoke to. Chapters 2 and 3 should be of interest to anyone who wants an account of what is wrong with OSI and whether or not it is getting better over time. While Chapters 4 to 6 on contestation often employ discussion which is more specific to heads and teachers, the general arguments apply more widely.

It is also hoped that the book will be relevant to educators in other countries. One reason for this is that many trends are similar in other countries, if rarely as intense. For instance, Apple and Beane (1999: xi–xii) have written about the USA in comparison to England:

> Think of it: no 'league tables'; no pre-specified national curriculum or national testing programme, somewhat fewer worries about image in the face of a competitive school market. Yet this totally romanticizes the situation that [US] educators face, for the differences are minor compared with the over-whelming similarities ... .

Moreover, since Apple and Beane were writing the US has introduced 'No Child Left Behind' (NCLB), a tough target setting and testing regime which brings it more into line with England's extreme performative environment (Hursh 2005). It is also important to note that OSI has been actively promoted internationally by English government officials and academics (e.g. DfEE 2000). This means that some policy importation from England will be difficult to avoid for other English-speaking nations, especially smaller nations, which are usually 'borrowers' rather than 'lenders' of policy.[1] On the other hand, the account here may be useful because England provides a great example to other countries of how *not* to proceed. Indeed that seems to be exactly how Welsh and Scottish policy-makers view England at times, for instance by pointedly turning away from SATs testing.

A more general reason this book should be relevant to international readers is that apart from the Gale and Densmore (2003) and Sachs (2003) texts already mentioned, there are few texts which focus on ways practitioners can respond critically to policy. Although – and in some ways because – it is closely concerned with a particular schooling context, I hope that those in other countries will find the discussion here helpful for reflecting on which education policies need challenging or subverting in their own setting and how this might occur. Indeed an encouraging conclusion of this book is that even in a strongly performative schooling environment like England's, practitioners can still find some room to contest reform if they want to. If this is the case, there will certainly be possibilities for useful action elsewhere as well.

2 Always winter and never Christmas

'The White Witch? Who is she?'
'Why it is she who has all Narnia under her thumb. It's she who makes it always winter. Always winter and never Christmas; think of that!'
(from *The Lion, the Witch and the Wardrobe* by C.S. Lewis)

Since it was elected in 1997, New Labour's education policy discourse for schools has centred on what Hatcher (1998) has called Official School Improvement (OSI). OSI has involved a market, managerial, performative and increasingly privatized approach to education which New Labour has vigorously promoted (see Ball *et al.* 2002; Docking 2000; Tomlinson 2005 for good overviews). It emphasizes testing, target setting, inspection, performance management and managerial school leadership as well as a feverish level of activity around Ofsted inspections, the programmes of the NCSL and initiatives like Specialist and Beacon schools, Excellence in Cities and City Academies.

In political terms of dominating media debate about education and staying ahead of public opposition, OSI has generally been very successful. Some reasons for this are:

- OSI's emphasis on 'standards not structures', that is, on finding 'what works', rather than going for wholesale changes in school organization. This has allowed New Labour to avoid difficult debates about 'structures', for instance the continuing dominance of the public (private) school system.
- OSI's general busyness. Along with key policies inherited from the Conservatives, OSI has involved numerous add-ons, schemes, special programmes and pilots. In its first term, New Labour seemed to announce a new initiative every week. By having so many initiatives it has both grabbed headlines and left possible critics struggling to keep up. For instance

the impact of many initiatives remains poorly researched because researchers have had to focus on some initiatives (e.g. Education Action Zones – EAZ's) at the expense of others (e.g. Excellence in Cities – EiC).

- OSI has been a constantly moving target. New Labour has been willing to quietly modify or discontinue OSI initiatives if they are judged a political liability.
- OSI has emphasized numbers. New Labour has had the achievement statistics or purported to have the achievement statistics to support its success in improving schools and against these it is hard to make a case for more qualitative concerns about the impact of OSI.
- OSI has co-opted some academics. For instance the Standards and Effectiveness Unit (SEU) of the DfES which has driven many OSI reforms was set up and run over New Labour's first term by one academic specializing in school improvement (Michael Barber) and taken over in its second term by another (David Hopkins).[1]

At the same time OSI has often been criticized in a range of more and less fundamental ways including:

- concerns about the way OSI has been put into practice in schools;
- concerns about whether OSI will reach its stated outcomes;
- concerns about OSI generating inequitable or perverse outcomes; and
- concerns about OSI's relevance.

This chapter considers OSI from each of these four perspectives. It is important at the outset to enter the caveat that the situation is nearly always more complex than can be portrayed in the space available here. For instance Ball *et al.* (2002: 19) have commented that 'Almost every generalization about the enactment and effects of Open Enrolment involves some kind of significant inaccuracy.' There is also clearly a risk of both 'golden-ageism' and overdeterminism here. It is therefore important to acknowledge that the welfarist schooling of previous decades was not wholly just and equitable, that many features of OSI under New Labour were inherited from the Conservatives rather than being generated by New Labour and that managerial reforms have not been simply taken up and 'implemented' by practitioners in any straight-forward way. Yet a continuing values 'drift' in education has clearly gone hand in hand with OSI. What this means is that what was considered unacceptable yesterday has often become less so today.

Criticisms (1) – OSI in practice

The ways in which OSI is put into practice in schools and LEAs can be subjected to various kinds of critique. Evaluation reports of DfES initiatives often note 'implementation' problems but since the remit for evaluators does not usually allow a fundamental critique, these discussions are typically fairly restrained. However interviews with practitioners often signal more serious difficulties. In this section I draw primarily on an interview with 'Mr Ramsay', a service manager in the inner-London borough of 'Wyeham'. The interview was undertaken in 2003 as part of an EU-funded research project 'Changes in Regulation Modes and Social Reproduction of Inequalities in Education Systems: A European Comparison' (Ball *et al.*, forthcoming; Thrupp *et al.* 2003; Thrupp *et al.* 2004). At the outset Mr Ramsay said that he agreed with the broad intent of OSI but was concerned with the way policy was translated into practice:

> 'When actually somebody sits down and goes through what the policy is and how it's meant to join up nationally, then it makes sense ... it was obviously very clever people that have it all worked out. The problem is policy into practice is a huge issue. You know, you could have a policy like Excellence In Cities, no-one's going to argue with that on principle. But how are you going to achieve that in schools?'

He argued that policy fragmentation, incoherence and monitoring requirements created huge difficulties for working with OSI and being held accountable for it. First there was the complexity of dealing with the numerous initiatives in the 'Standards Fund', all of which came with their own accountability requirements:

'What is interesting now is that people come in from HMI and so on, and they say "you are not actually working in a coordinated way". And we say "No, it's quite tricky". And we're just talking here about one funding stream, we're not talking about SRB, we're not talking about EMAG, we're not talking about leadership behaviour grant or improvement budget, we're not talking about all those other funding streams, all with their own accountabilities. [EiC] is a separate little section within the DfES. Separate people. Everyone's got to produce their plans, everyone's got to produce their annual accounts and their annual reports. … And most of the pots of money have run out. … So it's an absolute bureaucratic nightmare to try and make sense of it and bring it all together. It does rankle when you get slammed for not making sense of it, and not doing it in a coordinated way.'

One of the reasons that being held accountable was seen as unfair by Mr Ramsay was that in many cases arrangements are negotiated by schools directly with central government, with LEAs having little say:

'The problem with the Beacon Schools is that they are responsible to the DfES, they report to the DfES, they apply to the DfES, yet we're responsible for integrating them into the Borough for local Education Development Plans and all the rest of it, so there's certain tensions there. If you actually want to sort it out so they play an integral part of Wyeham and beyond, well, shouldn't they apply through us, and we'll go through the community plan with them and all that? Obviously not. So that doesn't work, so we're being hit with the accountability for the programmes, and making sure they're effective, but the schools don't see themselves as accountable to us, they see themselves as accountable to the DfES.'

Other problems had to do with the language of policy, and perceived lack of feasibility:

'I don't think "gifted" is a good term to use … Because it's a very loaded term, not just for teachers, for the general public. … But that's come straight from Number Ten [New Labour's policy unit]. Imported from America. But I think a bit of consultation with schools, really, on the nomenclature would have really solved a lot of those problems.

It's one of those DfES programmes that's basically "on the hoof", put in, very little consultation beforehand. Um, of course, financially it's not possible.'

In some cases the perceived problems were sourced to the nature of the DfES. For instance Mr Ramsay referred to a well-known case of 'spin' in New Labour's first term when education spending was announced but it was not made clear that this was actually money already announced:[2] 'there has been a real increase but, of course, there needed to be because of the massive [previous] under-investment'. He also talked about lack of communication within the DfES leading to mixed messages at the local level. Here he cited one local school about which the DfES had major concerns but was nevertheless recommending for a DfES award:

'Different section of the DfES presumably! So ... when you go to the DfES and they say, "what are you going to do about these schools", you say, "you've just given them an award, for being brilliant". You can't make it up!'

Mr Ramsay argued that the DfES's administration costs were spiralling because 'one of the things that they are doing is generating work for people like me to say, you know, "where's your action plan, where's your evaluation, where's your annual report"'. Added to this was the focus within the DfES on generic New Public Management skills rather than sector-specific knowledge:

'What they do is move people around. And the guy that was working on Excellence Challenge, you know, started to listen to us, we got to work with him, very reasonable, felt we were moving forward, he got promotion to Ministry of Agriculture, Fisheries and Food, you know. That's the way it works – get a promotion and you'll be off to the Department of Trade and Industry or the Department of Work and Pensions, and then you've got to start all over again because you've been in the DfES for three years. So, there is an issue to me, not of recruitment and retention, but of the ability of the DfES. People are forever moving around.'

Lack of genuine consultation was seen as a key part of the problem:

'You need to talk to people in schools about what is practical. Because one thing is that DFES people don't seem to understand that people in schools are generally teaching. And when they're not teaching, they're marking, and if they're not marking they're writing reports, or actually they're having a cup of coffee and a cigarette in the staff room, because even then they'll be talking about kids, that dominates their lives. And so [the DfES] get frustrated because they call a school for about two or three days, and they can't get the person they want. Well, you actually need to approach the person and organize a meeting after school or whatever. You come up with the policy, and then you try to translate it into practice, you've got to take into account that deadlines in schools come and go because you're dealing with kids, and kids are immediate, and you've got to be there for them and deal with that there and then. And, you know, you've got all the paperwork and all the rest of it. The reason schools actually manage it is because there are some fantastic people in there.'

Yet in the end, Mr Ramsay's concerns are more about being on the receiving end of bad policy than about mere 'implementation' problems. Moreover while he provides an especially trenchant critique of OSI, his views were echoed by many others interviewed in Wyeham. However not all of those interviewed laid the blame with the government. For instance, Mr Eatwell, another service manager, argued that the manner in which reform was taken up by school and LEA staff was the key issue:

'The weakness of [OSI] is that locally it is not always interpreted sufficiently well. So you have things like national literacy and the National Numeracy Strategy which I think are excellent, I think they are really powerful models, and they are at their most powerful when the LEA and the schools interpret them in a way that fits the schools. If they just take the materials and apply them without thinking through, "how do our pupils and how do our parents need to be helped by these?", if they don't do that [the models] just don't work so well.'

Yet even here there were different perspectives on where the problem really lay. To Mr Simmons, a third service manager, part of the problem with local implementation was that it could have the surface appearance of being equitable when the degree to which schools could really respond to policy was reliant on the make-up of the governing body. Since this varied considerably between schools, it was inevitable that 'unevenness' developed and 'those who have' were allowed to have more.

Criticisms (2) – OSI's stated outcomes

Another type of criticism of OSI is that it fails in its own terms, i.e. to meet its own stated outcomes of improved student achievement, an economically competitive workforce, and reduced social exclusion and unemployment.

It has often been claimed that OSI has produced results in terms of reducing educational under-attainment. However claims of improved achievement need to be interrogated carefully. Wiliam (2001) pointed out that curricula are always changing and that what is actually taught in schools changes even if the 'official' curriculum is not changed. 'For example, the pressure on primary schools to improve their Key Stage 2 results in English, mathematics and science has increased markedly in recent years. Understandably, therefore, schools have increased the attention given to these subjects over recent years to improve students' results on the Key Stage 2 tests' (p. 8). He went on to argue:

> Successive governments have created a situation in which policy is currently based on assumptions that are not merely unsupported by evidence but just plain wrong, and rising test scores demonstrate little more than teachers' increasing abilities to teach to the tests, and to the power of high-stakes tests to distort the curriculum. (p. 14)

Different kinds of evidence support the 'teaching to the test' thesis. For instance at Key Stage (KS) 2 level there has been the phenomena that Maths and English results rose steadily from 1995–2000 but then plateaued. Moreover, over the period when Maths and English results were rising, the other core subject, Science, rose at a similar rate. This was despite having no 'science hour' – in fact teachers reported they were teaching less science because of the 'literacy hour' and 'daily maths lesson'. So the similar rates of improvement for Maths, Science and English are unlikely to have been because of government strategies (because there were none in Science) but because teachers were getting better at teaching to the tests.[3]

Tymms (2004) uses results from several different studies and an analysis of the standard-setting procedures to provide a comprehensive critique of the officially reported gains in achievement at KS 2. His key conclusion is that national testing has failed to accurately monitor standards over time. He gives various reasons for this, including the following problems:

- statistical procedures were faulty and not corrected until 2000/01;
- test data have been used in a very high stakes fashion so that the pressure created makes it hard to interpret the data. 'Teaching test technique must surely have contributed to some of the rise, as must teaching to the test' (p. 492);
- the form of the national tests has changed over time;
- curricula have inevitably changed and therefore so has test content.

New Labour's claims about improvements being made at the school level with previously 'failing schools' with low levels of student achievement (e.g. DfEE 2001; DfES 2001) are also problematic. First, some of the percentage gains being trumpeted are actually very modest and in many cases unlikely to be significant. Second, teaching to the test will probably be even more marked in 'failing' schools because of the more intense performative pressures on them. Third, some of the evidence for success comes from Ofsted data but it is apparent that Ofsted's assessments of schools have been highly politicized, socially decontextualized and methodologically flawed (Boothroyd *et al.* 1997; Mansell 2000a). Indeed Fitz-Gibbon and Stephenson (1996: 17) have argued that Ofsted's methods have 'failed to meet even the most elementary standards with regard to sampling, reliability and validity' (see also Chapter 3). Finally, official case studies of improving schools are usually just too tidy to ring true. They provide little sense of the day-to-day struggles and messy tensions which more independent accounts of 'failing schools' point up (e.g. Davies 2000; Wallace 2001a and 2001b).

A second aim of New Labour policy has been to create an economically competitive workforce. One concern related to this is that the prescribed curriculum often crowds out opportunities for students to exercise their personal creativity. As Jill, a teacher we interviewed in a Wyeham secondary school, put it:

> 'On the one hand there seems to be this ever increasing emphasis on results, statistics, exam performance, and that puts a lot of pressure on teachers. It seems [to demand] just to focus more and more on just delivering that. And yet there's also this paradoxical focus of encouraging schools to be more creative, to develop things which are extra-curricular, cross-curricular, giving opportunities for children to be creative, and to just look and build new links and give new opportunities. There are opposing forces but for a lot of teachers, it just seems to give a pressure which is just irreconcilable with, you know, "well, we've just got to keep them in the classroom for fifteen minutes", "we've got to get the curriculum delivered".'

Lauder (cited in Ball 1999: 202) has argued that by encouraging a narrow, prescribed approach to the taught curriculum, OSI may lead to 'trained incapacity' in the workforce and hence reduce rather than enhance national economic competitiveness. He has also noted that little is known about the impact of repeated testing on students' motivation or their desire for further education after compulsory schooling (Brown and Lauder 2002).

A third official goal, reducing social exclusion and unemployment, also seems unlikely to be addressed by OSI. Brown and Lauder (2002) note that one reason for this is that New Labour's own targets allow 20 per cent of students to perform below the expected average of each age group tested, the effect of this target alone is likely to ensure that 20 per cent with few skills will become part of a group of early school leavers classified as neither in education or employment. Nor can it be assumed that any overall increase in the education levels of a population will lead to better employment prospects for those most at risk of 'social exclusion' (or anyone else for that matter). As Wolf (2002) has illustrated, this is because of the positional nature of education within the labour market. She concludes:

> Clearly, people without good levels of basic academic skills are at a permanent disadvantage in our world. But if there is one thing which … [is] clear, it is that education is a 'positional good' (as the economists call it) – one which gains much of its value from whether you have more than other people – and is not just about acquiring skills in some absolute way. The rewards your education bring are as much to do with being labelled a 'top' or a 'near-the-top' sort of person as they are to do with the sort of curriculum you studied. *And not everyone can be top.* So … secondary education becomes segmented as it becomes universal; universities form themselves into even clearer hierarchies; and fourteen year olds who are failing academically quite rationally lose motivation. Pile more and more education on top of what is already there and you end up with the same segmentation, the same positioning and even greater problems of cost and quality. (Wolf 2002: 251, her emphasis)

Wolf also argues that vocational education is both expensive and inefficient in terms of promoting social inclusion. One reason for this raised by Brown and Lauder (2002) is that training for those in the poor work segment of the labour market occurs in a vacuum since firms that make their profit out of cheap labour are unlikely to embrace vocational training because they don't need it. They cite Crouch, Finegold and Sako (1999: 75) who point out that most studies show that the training resources of firms are concentrated on those already highly educated.

Criticisms (3) – OSI's inequitable or perverse outcomes

Concerns about the harmful social and educational effects of OSI have often been raised by academic and practitioner critics. These effects include polarized schools and communities, a narrowed educational focus and the loss of authenticity in schools, a reduction in the sociability of schools and communities, the commodification and marginalization of children, the distraction of existing teachers and school leaders, the discouragement of potential teachers and school leaders and the undermining of more progressive policies. As I discuss these problems below, it will be apparent that it is often the combination of policies which is harmful – the fact that self-management is occurring in a market context, for instance.

New Labour has followed the Conservatives to emphasize the importance of parents being allowed a 'choice' of schools to suit their child's educational needs as well as their need for information on student achievement to inform that choice. It is also increasingly opening up 'diversity' through specialist and beacon schools (Tomlinson 2005). Yet because parental decision-making around school choice is often dominated by concern about social reproduction or mobility, studies which have investigated parental choice of schools in educational markets have found that among the public, low socio-economic schools (low SES schools) are widely considered inferior to middle-class schools. Overall it seems that most parents, regardless of ethnic or class group, believe that attending high SES schools advantages children, even if their own children are not able to attend such schools.

The predictable effect of policies which open up choice and diversity is that high SES schools tend to become thoroughly oversubscribed and can choose their students, while low SES schools struggle to maintain their rolls and have to take all students to survive. High SES schools which get to choose their students tend to favour white, middle class, able students who will enhance the positional standing of the school. Less favoured schools become dominated by the students left behind – those from working-class backgrounds, minority groups, recent refugees, those who have been previously excluded and those with special needs. As a result, the development of quasi-market relations between schools is likely to intensify the social polarization of school intakes (Ball 2003; Noden 2000). [4]

Like 'choice', self-management is a quasi-market policy inasmuch as it is intended to allow schools to respond to market imperatives and the incentive to do this is per capita funding which ties school funding to the numbers of students on roll. Because of this, and differential contributions from families in richer and poorer areas, schools also become polarized between those which are relatively well resourced (in terms of material resources, physical plant, staffing levels and so on) and those which are not. For 'unpopular' schools, 'self-management' can become a matter of serious and continuing budget constraints. Schools are also polarized in terms of academic status as reflected in league tables and Ofsted inspections because of the differential impact of family background, school mix, school resources and staffing. This then generates inequalities in the ability of schools to attract staff. Apart from the desire to 'make a difference', why would teachers want to work in schools which are often badly resourced, under heavy surveillance as 'failing' and perhaps likely to close?

These forms of polarization are mutually reinforcing so that, as the quasi-market develops over time, it may be difficult for unpopular schools in working-class areas not to enter a spiral of decline (become 'sink schools') or indeed for middle-class schools not to be popular and successful. The increasing number of interventions directed at 'failing schools' are intended to solve this problem and they do provide extra resources (DfES 2001; Thrupp 2001a). However, the impact of such resources is likely to be limited so long as policies of choice and per capita funding remain in place. Moreover, polarized schools may also help to create a more unequal society by having an impact on residential segregation as over time people increasingly choose to live away from schools that have become unpopular. The effects of the 'diversity' policies also often adds to the problem of polarization. This occurs between schools as a result of moving away from a comprehensive model to the establishment of specialist or charter schools which have a selective element. Differentiation also occurs within schools through the promotion of setting and gifted, able or talented programmes which are usually disproportionately taken up by white middle-class families who can exercise their cultural and material advantages in pursuit of a 'better education'. Meanwhile, the market discourages within-school programmes for students who are a liability in market terms such as those with special educational needs.

OSI has also reduced the educational breadth of schools both directly through curriculum prescription and indirectly through its emphasis on outcomes, the intensification of workloads and the impact of market pressures. First, there can be little doubt that curriculum prescription geared to white middle-class interests helps to foster rather than reduce inequality (Connell 1994). Alternative approaches to teaching which might better suit groups other than the white middle class get squeezed out. It is not just marginalized groups which suffer. A highly prescriptive focus as illustrated by the Literacy and Numeracy strategies reduces time spent not only on only subjects often regarded as curriculum 'frills' (for instance art, drama, physical education) but even subjects long regarded as being curriculum 'basics', for instance science and geography.

There is also now much evidence to show how increased emphasis on assessment against narrow criteria – whether through testing, target setting, inspection or performance management – also reduces the curriculum as the 'tail wags the dog': schools and teachers are encouraged to teach to the test/target/inspection/ performance management appraisal. Because of this there really is a joyless sense of 'Always winter and never Christmas' under the highly performative OSI regime. For instance Gillborn and Youdell discuss what they call the 'A-to-C economy' in which 'almost every aspect of school life is re-evaluated for its possible contribution to the headline statistic of the proportion of pupils attaining at least 5 higher grade GCSE passes' (Gillborn and Youdell 2000: 12). The pressure to perform leads to impression management by way of fabrication. For instance, prior to Ofsted inspections teachers create artefacts and ritualistic displays of their work and their teaching and assessment values and practices are increasingly led by Ofsted requirements. Ball (2001) illustrates many forms of fabrication which occur in the 'performing school' through the routine selection (or manipulation) of statistics and indicators, the stage management of events and the kinds of accounts that schools and individuals construct around themselves.

With lots of administration related to accountability, OSI also leads to intensification of workloads and this in itself reduces the curriculum. An important loss are the informal activities which lead to mutual learning and improved relationships between teachers and students and which can therefore be 'traded on' in delivering the formal curriculum, for instance teachers sitting in a classroom during a lunch hour just 'shooting the breeze' or 'having a laugh' with a group of students, or running an after school club for students centred on some personal enthusiasm, e.g. chess or painting. OSI has led to a decline in such 'organic' extra-curricular activity as teachers struggle to find the time to manage their formal workloads, let alone anything extra (Gewirtz 2002).

Another indirect pressure to narrow the curriculum comes from the market. Schools may be self-managing but if they do not keep up their market share they can be in big trouble. Consequently even the autonomy experienced by more popular higher SES schools will be limited to paths which are likely to reinforce their continuing popularity. Indeed the problem with market pressures is that, because so many parents are looking for the style of education associated with the socially elite, the market often has a conservatizing effect in the direction of a traditional grammar school model rather than encouraging exciting innovations as is often theorized (Glatter, Woods and Bagley 1997). Thus diversity tends to be of particular kinds which still largely fit this traditional model, for instance the curricula foci associated with the specialist schools programme. It is very difficult in a market context to pursue genuine alternatives. All of this limits what teachers do and what students learn. Thus Gewirtz (2002) reports a general decline in the vitality and creativity of teaching and less opportunity for progressive practices.

At various levels OSI also reduces the sociability of schools and communities. Relationships between heads and their staff have become more bureaucratic and distant. Reay (1998) examined staff relationships across a number of London schools, and argues that managerialism has bought a shift in values in which senior staff have become more powerful and controlling and teachers are increasingly viewed as just a means to the end of increased student performance. She points in particular to headteachers engineering teacher compliance, and reducing dissent through the use of staff appointments, staff training, reference to school effectiveness literature, and in some cases, more overtly aggressive approaches such as bullying tactics in meetings. While Reay indicates strong senior management team collegiality, the social distance between them and their staff was growing. Reay also points to strong regulation and surveillance of teachers, and of relationships between teachers and senior managers being 'pared down and perfunctory' within the new managerialism, while Mahony, Menter and Hextall (2004) found that the introduction of Performance Related Pay (PRP) served to further disillusion rather than motivate most teachers. OSI also leads to increasing tensions between teaching staff. Gewirtz (2002) found a decline in sociability because of time shortage and because teachers were meeting less about teaching matters and more often about management concerns. Reay found that the schools were marked by increasing inter-department competition, with an ethos of divide and rule created by competitive bidding and intense competition for success.

Meanwhile the market generates the view of parents as 'consumers' rather than 'partners' and this creates anxiety among teachers over satisfying parents and among parents over their children's education. The anti-social element of educational quasi-markets extends out into communities and cities. As parents drive their children to schools across town, cities become less pleasant places to live, with more traffic congestion and air pollution. In some neighbourhoods children now go to many different schools rather than just one or two and the notion of the local school as a centre of community has all but broken down.

A very disturbing aspect of OSI is the way it has encouraged those in schools to think of children not in terms of their own needs but in terms of what advantages they can bring to the positional well-being of the school. This commodification of children occurs both in their initial recruitment and in the management of them once in the school. OSI encourages schools to recruit bright, middle-class 'able' children and to avoid taking on 'expensive' SEN and excluded pupils wherever possible (Bagley, Woods and Glatter 2001). This reorientation of schools is encouraged by government schemes which are aimed at offering special programmes for the 'gifted and talented'. To Bagley and colleagues these developments produce a 'pronounced misalignment between the policy emphasis and market strategies of schools and the consumer interests of, in particular, parents of children with SEN' (Bagley, Woods and Glatter 2001: 306).

Once in schools, children are further commodified and (some) are marginalized through decisions around setting and testing. In one of the most damning critiques of OSI, Gillborn and Youdell (2000) note the occurrence of 'educational triage' where decisions are made to focus on some students at the expense of others depending on whether or not they are seen to have the potential to enhance their school's position in the examination league tables. Beckett (2005: 9) notes that some schools 'routinely sacrifice the best interests of pupils' in order to shine in exam league tables:

> The worst offenders – though not the only ones – are Britain's 165 grammar schools. At the age of 11 grammar schools select the brightest children from miles around. Then, when pupils reach the age of 16, the school often has another trawl, discarding pupils who will not bring them higher up the A-level league tables, and poaching a very few of the best and brightest whom they may have missed at the age of 11.

OSI often distracts from both an instructional and social justice focus. Gewirtz (2002) points to resentment and accumulated stress among teachers because of an increased emphasis on recording and monitoring student progress, which was perceived by teachers as a distraction from the real work of teaching.

Managerialism is often forced on self-managing schools by central dictate, for example the requirement for schools to undergo Ofsted inspections or to adopt PRP. Managerial solutions can also be promoted in education by central government, for instance through the content of NCSL programmes (see Chapter 4). More generally, however, OSI opens up schools to managerialism because school leader and others need to find ways of managing schools and selling potentially unpopular reforms to their staff. In casting around for ideas, they are inevitably exposed (along with more clearly educational thinking) to generic managerial ideas which flow from the wider policy and business environment: the head as CEO!

Schools have become more concerned with institutional survival and thus issues around budget, roll size and make-up and school image. This preoccupation is not just limited to working-class schools where survival is a genuine problem. Even popular schools dominated by children from middle-class families are preoccupied by a concern to retain and enhance their position in the league tables. From a critical perspective market and managerial distractions, however important for institutional survival, represent an opportunity cost in terms of expense, time and energy which could be used on instructional and equity concerns. For instance, it has been estimated that an Ofsted inspection costs a school £20,000 pounds and there are further costs related to LEA inspections and school marketing (Gewirtz 2000; Hood *et al.* 1999). Meanwhile many teachers clearly find Ofsted inspections and Key Stage testing time-consuming and stressful (Jeffrey and Woods 1998). Gillborn and Youdell (2000: 222) conclude that 'it is time this level of activity was refocused towards the achievement of social justice'.

Another insidious effect of OSI is the discouragement of potential teachers and school leaders and consequent recruitment problems. While it would be inaccurate to see OSI as entirely responsible for teacher shortages in England (other factors such as the nature of the graduate labour market and changing student cultures also come in to play), there is little doubt that the intensification of workload, increased accountability and perceived deprofessionalization of teachers' work has made teaching a less popular graduate occupation. To some extent the same is true of school leadership. Because of managerial changes in the role of heads and their increasing distance from staff, it seems that most teachers cannot see themselves in the role (Thornton 2002a). On the other hand, those of managerial leaning may find the role more attractive. Both trends may help to bring about a 'new breed' of more managerial heads to replace the welfarist heads who have retired or left as OSI has gathered momentum (see also Chapter 5).

A final perversity of OSI is that it leads to the crowding out of central steering of the 'right' kind, in other words that which could have an impact on social justice. For instance, Gewirtz (2002: 139) notes that until recently there was 'little explicit expectation within Ofsted's documentation that schools would attend to social justice issues'. Governments can now use the excuse that schools are self-managing in order not to intervene on equity grounds. Privatization also clearly limits the ability of the state to intervene. Another difficulty is that strong acknowledgement of the impact of schools' social contexts collides with OSI's central tenets. It is the ability of the state to hold that school staff are clearly responsible for the success or failure of schools which supports its use of quasi-markets and forms of managerial accountability. The OSI framework does not adequately capture the impact of social context on schools in a way that can produce more useful and progressive policy, for instance policy which is really attuned to the needs of working-class and minority students.

Criticisms (4) – OSI's relevance

A further broad criticism of OSI is that it fails to address the burning social, political and environmental issues of the day. Even with the numerous distractions of modern life, it is hard not to recognize that we live in a world of serious, interconnected and often intensifying social, environmental and political problems. These include vast inequalities of wealth and power, lack of religious and ethnic tolerance and serious degradation of air, land, forests and seas – problems manifested locally, nationally and globally. Most of us are able to put some distance between ourselves and the worst effects of these problems: for instance in the UK it is the poor who suffer the worst effects of pollution.[5] Yet no-one is entirely unaffected by problems elsewhere, a point well illustrated by the events of 9/11 and subsequent bombings in Europe, as well as by the tsunami which hit the shores of countries around the Indian Ocean in December 2004.

As we contemplate an increasingly uncertain global future, the kinds of social, environmental and political problems mentioned above surely represent such fundamental human concerns that an awareness of them ought to be, in an age-appropriate way, a major aim of the school curriculum. But time to build such understanding – what might be called the development of social, environmental and political literacy – is another kind of education crowded out by OSI.

The irrelevance of OSI results from both the taught and hidden curriculum. For instance, while there are elements of the prescribed school curriculum which seem to be addressing wider social, environmental and political concerns, for example PSHE, citizenship and geography, the sheer paucity of curriculum time given over to these issues compared to 'basics' like literacy and numeracy remains a key issue. What is actually taught is also often an individualized analysis rather than one which considers the structural and political forces which lead to individuals acting in the way they do. There is also the problem of the 'hidden curriculum' whereby schools are not required or enabled to 'walk the walk' as well as 'talk the talk' under OSI. OSI does not encourage schools to operate in ways which are just, democratic and environmentally aware. I have already noted that OSI has created less democratic staff relations and encouraged schools to commodify students rather than value them as learners regardless of their social backgrounds and academic progress. Indeed the progressive moments which exist in the curriculum under OSI may often have a legitimating role than anything else.

To conclude this chapter, the OSI agenda within which schools are immersed takes up most of their energies. It creates numerous problems for 'implementation', fails to achieve its own stated outcomes, creates perverse and inequitable outcomes and requires schools, from a wider social, political and environmental point of view, to 'fiddle while Rome burns'. However, it could be argued that as OSI has been improving in recent times, practitioners would be better to go with it than use up their precious energies on trying to contest it. Chapter 3 investigates this possibility.

3 Just one piece of Turkish Delight?

'Please, please' said Edmund suddenly, 'please couldn't I have just one piece of Turkish Delight to eat on the way home?' 'No, no,' said the Queen with a laugh, 'you must wait till next time.' While she spoke, she signalled to the dwarf to drive on, but as the sledge swept out of sight, the Queen waved to Edmund, calling out 'Next time!, Next time!' (from *The Lion, the Witch and the Wardrobe* by C.S. Lewis)

For practitioners and academics alike, going against the flow of education policy is nearly always more difficult than going with it. For this reason, even if the thrust of the critique outlined in Chapter 2 is accepted, it would be tempting to support OSI if it could be demonstrated to be changing in ways which would allow for more progressive activities by heads and teachers in the future. And indeed a refreshing change of direction does seem to be signalled in some recent policy, most obviously in *Excellence and Enjoyment* (DfES 2003), the Primary Strategy's initial policy document. The possibility of a shift in OSI therefore needs to be explored while bearing in mind that we may risk grasping at straws. Appearances can also be deceptive: careful analysis is needed.

Here I begin by looking at the Primary Strategy and critiques of the claim that it is opening up the curriculum before turning in greater detail to the work of Ofsted whose inspections have been a longstanding feature of OSI but are often thought to have changed for the better in recent years. My discussion of these two areas of policy will illustrate that while there is clearly *some* truth in the argument that OSI is opening up the curriculum, there is certainly no sign yet of it shifting in such fundamental ways that it need not be contested.

The Primary Strategy

Rejecting the narrowing of the curriculum noted in the last chapter, the Primary Strategy argues that 'High standards and a broad and rich curriculum go hand in hand' (Primary Strategy homepage, www.standards.dfes.gov.uk/primary). Schools are now being encouraged to 'design broad and rich curricula which make the most of links between different areas and provide opportunities for children to have a wide range of learning experiences' (DfES 2003). Supporting this development is *Learning and Teaching in the Primary Years*, a set of new professional development resources. These resources are noteworthy for being recommended rather than obligatory:

> The materials are not intended to replace existing good practice. Schools will decide when and how – and even if – they use these resources. As a professional learning community you will have discussed your priorities and will have evaluated the impact of the work you have already done on learning and teaching. You will therefore already know where you still have areas for development. These materials will supplement what you are already doing and suggest how you might explore further areas. If your current approach is raising achievement across the curriculum and is providing a broad and rich curriculum you are probably already doing many of the things in these units. In these circumstances you may wish to use them as a resource for staff meetings on those occasions when you revisit and review key areas of learning and teaching. (From Primary Strategy Website)

Also supporting the development are Primary Strategy Learning Networks which are small groups of schools, typically five to eight schools, who collaborate around some teaching or learning area or issue. Examples given on the Primary Strategy website include problem-solving in mathematics, boys' writing, modern foreign languages in Year 3, linking best practice in literacy with language teaching and learning, and speaking and listening for children for whom English is an additional language. One strength of this initiative is a two-stage funding process with some initial funding given to support the planning of the network before the main funding is provided to actually run it (DfES 2004a).

All this sounds promising but there are important limits to the policy too. Most obviously, although SATs tests have been dropped at KS1 in favour of teacher assessments, this is not the case at KS2, although at this level schools now set their own targets with LEA targets being set afterwards, rather than the other way around as happened previously. Less apparent, the new freedoms offered by the Primary Strategy itself are often likely to be illusory. Alexander (2004: 14) warns that 'The Strategy's intentions are more opaque and contradictory than at first sight they seem, especially when the document is set alongside other statements of current education policy.' In particular he argues that while *Excellence and Enjoyment* emphasizes that the Literacy and Numeracy strategies are not statutory, mere awareness of this will not free teachers to innovate:

> Legally, the claims about what is and is not statutory are correct, but how many teachers will take this as an invitation to reduce the time spent on literacy and numeracy in order to free time for the rest of the curriculum, knowing as they do how much hangs on the next round of literacy and numeracy targets. (Alexander 2004: 15)

Despite talk of children's entitlement to a rich, broad and balanced set of learning experiences (DfES 2003, para. 3.1), curriculum 'basics' can still be expected to dominate:

> Many schools have all but given up on the original 1988 National Curriculum notion of children's absolute entitlement to a genuinely broad curriculum. ... The Primary Strategy does nothing to alleviate the problem ... but by ring fencing the Literacy and Numeracy Strategies it ensures that the listed Curriculum II initiatives – creativity, the languages strategy, the PE and sport strategy, music – though separately admirable, will in conjunction have a hard time of it. ... In a Primary Strategy called 'Excellence and Enjoyment', it is made very clear that the 3Rs again provide the excellence and the rest delivers the enjoyment: Curriculum I and II yet again. (DfES 2003: 20)

Alexander highlights 'the Strategy's doublespeak on professional autonomy' and its 'ambiguity of intent – a desire to be seen to be offering freedom while in reality maintaining control':

Against the ostensible offer of autonomy, we have the continuing pressure of testing, targets and performance tables and the creeping hegemonization of the curriculum by the Literacy and Numeracy Strategies, with three-part lessons, interactive whole class teaching and plenaries soon to become a template for the teaching of everything. (DfES 2003: 15)

Hatcher (2005: 255) also argues that the Primary Strategy needs to be seen against the strengthening of two other key instruments of government control of headteachers and, through them, their staff:

One is Ofsted inspections, which will be shorter but sharper and more frequent. Furthermore, the category of 'satisfactory' lessons has been redefined as 'unsatisfactory'. The other is the pay and promotion of teachers. Headteachers have to review teachers on the main spine annually and only if they are graded 'satisfactory' can they move up the scale. After the threshold, promotion is selective because of limited school budgets and is dependent on headteachers judging staff as having 'grown professionally'.

All of this reminds us of the importance of seeing any initiative 'in the round' rather than viewing it in isolation and certainly it seems that the Primary Strategy is offering more than its associated OSI policies will sustain. Rather than signalling any general trend in OSI, the Primary Strategy may be more about trying to respond to the particular problem of public and professional unease about the narrowing and stultifying effects of SATs testing and target setting on the education of very young children. For instance, parents have often gone on national television to argue against SATs testing of their young children while support for a campaign against primary SATs testing run by the *Times Educational Supplement* (*TES*) in 2002 was a clear indicator of professional concern. Even so, New Labour seems to have only given way as little as possible. As noted above, SATs have been retained at the end of KS2 (when children are aged 10–11) where SATs testing is less controversial than the testing of 6–7 year olds at the end of KS1.

Ofsted[1]

Earlier I noted Hatcher's concerns about Ofsted 'undoing' the positive effects of the Primary Strategy and yet Ofsted is another area where practitioners and the media are often taking the view that New Labour policy is becoming more progressive over time. For instance, reflecting its surveys which indicate that since 2001 Ofsted has grown in popularity among teachers (e.g. Canovan 2002a) the *TES* has become more supportive of Ofsted (e.g. 'Keep the chief' 2001; 'Self-evaluation is their future' 2002); Shaw 2002a; Ryan 2004). Along the same lines, by 2002 the *Education Guardian* was introducing its online special report on Ofsted with the statement that 'Ofsted has been softening its stance towards schools' (*http://education.guardian.co.uk/schools/specialreports/*).

Nevertheless the following discussion of Ofsted will illustrate once again that policy can appear to be improving without really changing in any fundamental way. I begin by providing an overview of Ofsted under New Labour. Accepting that they are interrelated problems, I then look at Ofsted policy developments in relation to five issues: acknowledgement of social context, market forces and privatization, managerialism, performativity and curriculum prescription. In each case I distinguish between cases where a more searching or progressive stance seems to be being taken ('on the up') or apparently not ('the same or worse').

Ofsted under New Labour 1997–2004

In many ways Ofsted under the first term of New Labour (or more accurately until late 2000 while HMCI Chris Woodhead was still at the helm) was like Ofsted under the Conservatives but more severe. For instance, whereas between 1993 and 1997 Ofsted reviews put approximately 250 schools into special measures (Stark 1998), some 916 schools were placed in special measures over 1997–2001. New Labour made special measures part of a hierarchy of school failure which included 'serious weaknesses' and added clear consequences if a school did not improve quickly. Although the Conservatives closed some schools by putting pressure on LEAs, the School Standards and Framework Bill (1998) gave Ministers the power to directly close schools not responding to special measures. In June 1998 Education Secretary David Blunkett announced 'a tough new policy to stop prolonged failure in schools'. Schools in special measures would have to be turned around in two years. If not turned around, the schools would be closed or given a Fresh Start.

Under the Conservatives, Ofsted had had a key ideological role of 'turning up the heat' of neo-liberal school reform and Woodhead, who had been in the role of HCMI since 1994 clearly identified with the neo-liberal critics of education (Thrupp 1998). He took up New Labour's initial 'tough on schools' discourse (with its 'naming and shaming' of the 'worst' schools in Britain) with great vigour and sometimes with little real attention to inspection evidence.[2] As Lawton (2000: 5) put it 'In evaluating Ofsted, a distinction needs to be made between the methods used in the inspection process ... and the use made of the evidence drawn from inspections, including use made of data by Her Majesty's Chief Inspectors.' Yet in November 2000 Woodhead's relationship with the Blair government collapsed and he resigned. It seems likely that in an era of growing public concern about severe teacher shortages, his 'tough on teachers' persona became a liability for New Labour. Woodhead's conservative stance also repeatedly put him at logger-heads with senior education officials (Iredale 2004). There is no doubt his claims about incompetent teachers – he once claimed that at least 15,000 were failing – were deeply antagonistic.

The arrival of Woodhead's temporary replacement, Mike Tomlinson, in 2000 signalled the kinds of changes which might lead us to think Ofsted has improved over New Labour's second term. There was talk about more use of school self-evaluation and shorter 'light touch' inspections were introduced for 'successful' schools. In May 2001 measures were announced to reduce the bureaucratic burden of school inspections (Mansell 2001a). An independent adjudicator was appointed[3] and Tomlinson suggested only reviewing most schools every ten years, although this idea was then quickly quashed by David Blunkett and by Estelle Morris who took over from Blunkett as Education Secretary in June 2001. Against the background of accusations from Woodhead that they were going 'soft on standards' (Learner 2001a), Blunkett and

Morris wanted to continue the emphasis on failing schools, the latter declaring:

> It's not about moving to self-evaluation, it's not about 10-year inspection arrangements, it's not about more short inspections. It's about using our resources in a more directed way – concentrating those resources on those schools that are not performing well. (Cited in Mansell 2001b)

Nevertheless by September 2001 it was announced that Ofsted was consulting towards the 2003 introduction of new school inspections which would be 'soft-touch style but tough on standards' (Learner 2001b), while inspections of LEAs would change from 'rooting out failure' to a 'softer focus' on 'promoting excellence' (Kelly 2001). The main features would be shorter inspection for all primary schools, an end to grading individual teachers, pupil questionnaires, schools being able to select an area for inspection and more flexible inspection models to reflect differing school contexts. There was approval from the *TES* which argued Tomlinson should be made the next permanent head of Ofsted ('Keep the chief' 2001) and gave him quote of the week:

> I want an inspection system to be something we do with schools rather than to schools. I fully believe the inspection process is one that should be done with the school playing an active part rather than being a passive recipient. (Tomlinson, quoted in the *TES*, 14 September 2001)

Also bolstering its support, Ofsted increasingly expressed concern about wider policy developments including the value of specialist schools and the impact of staff shortages on primary schools (Ward 2001; Learner 2001c). These kinds of criticisms continued under David Bell's leadership after mid-2002. Along with its more usual comments on schools and LEAs, Ofsted has raised concerns about the staffing crisis in schools (Shaw 2002b), specialist schools (Shaw 2003a), privatization of LEAs (Slater 2003a), neglect of inner-city schools (Curtis 2003b), EiC (Brown 2003; Shaw 2003b), Curriculum 2000 (Shaw 2003b), EAZs (Shaw 2003c), primary school targets (Shaw and Slater 2003), ministers' fixation with targets in general (Shaw 2003d, 'Fixation with targets "damaging" teacher morale' 2003), pay inequality between school and FE teaching (Shaw 2003e) and primary strategy consultant leaders (Curtis 2004a; Slater 2004a).

In terms of Ofsted's approach to inspection, the period since 2001 has been marked by a number of shifts. In March 2002 it was announced that inspection resources would be focused on improving failing LEAs ('Inspectors to concentrate on poorly performing councils' (2002) despite the opposite messages of just a few months before. In April 2002, Ofsted announced that self-evaluation would be an important part of the post-2003 inspection framework, in line with Tomlinson but contradicting Estelle Morris's stance of less than a year earlier (Canovan 2002b). By May 2003, final details of the post-September school inspection arrangements were emerging. Short inspections (which only a fraction of schools received) were to be scrapped after complaints from heads that they were too superficial. But the average length of a standard inspection would shorten by several days and successful schools were to have up to six years between visits. Headteachers would rate aspects of schools' work from grade one (excellent) to grade seven (poor). Inspectors would then tailor their inspection to the information provided in the self-evaluation, spending less time examining areas where schools needed little assistance (Shaw 2003f).

The new 'light but rigorous' inspections were introduced in September 2003 but by the end of the autumn term an increased number of schools going into special measures was causing concern to teacher unions and MPs (Shaw 2003g; Abrams 2004). By February Ofsted was seeking to limit the damage to its newly 'reasonable' reputation. Bell argued in his annual report that failing an inspection could act as a catalyst to improvement and outweighed the negative effects suffered (Slater 2004b). He later complained about inspectors misleading headteachers by telling them that inspections had become more demanding (Stewart, Smith and Slater 2004). Eventually he admitted the new system was faulty and issued new guidance to try to reduce the number of failed inspections (Slater 2004c).

More fundamentally, Ofsted launched a consultation in February 2004 on new 'laser' inspections. The new approach would occur against a backdrop of budget cuts for many government depart-ments and agencies including Ofsted (Slater and Bushby 2004) and would be short, sharp and provide little notice:

> We're exchanging a searchlight for a laser. ... We want to check whether a school's central nervous system is working well, not map out its genomes. (Bell, cited in Slater 2004d)

By June 2004 initial details of the new inspection regime to be intro-duced from September 2005 were announced. Inspections would now take place at only a few days' notice. Small teams would visit for no more than two days. Inspections would occur more frequently, at least every three years. Self-evaluation would be at the centre of inspection. Reports would be short, about six pages. Schools would be required to amend their current development plan to take account of inspection (Slater and Shaw 2004).

Over New Labour's second term there has been continued critique of the impact of Ofsted in schools (Shaw *et al.* 2002) and in 2002 a group of 17 education professors led by Carol Fitz-Gibbon called for a Royal Commission into Ofsted and a halt to classroom obser-vations by inspectors until Ofsted was independently evaluated (Shaw 2002d). In response to this, but also in anticipation of the government's policy on inspection of public services (OPSR 2003), Ofsted commissioned an independent evaluation (Matthews and Sammons 2004). The Matthews and Sammons evaluation covers numerous issues but it is very much written for a policy rather than academic audience and provides only a constrained discussion of Ofsted's political role and its impact on schools. Indeed the evalu-ation reported that Ofsted has made a substantial contribution to the improvement of the education system (p. 153), although this was immediately disputed by teacher and headteacher organiza-tions (Macleod 2004b).

It is important to note the report's limited coverage of Ofsted inspection methodology. A key problem in inspection methodology are the causal assumptions required of inspectors. Indeed the post-September 2003 handbook tells inspectors they 'must evaluate effect rather than intention' (Ofsted 2003a: 111) but of course there is really no reliable way they can do this. Matthews and

Sammons do caution against 'attributing causality with certainty in the study of social and educational processes' but this is only done at the level of inferring an association between inspection and school improvement outcomes, not at the level of inspection methodology. Hence Martin Ward, deputy general secretary of the Secondary Heads Association, was able to dismiss the report by saying he did not believe the evidence for the good value of the Ofsted process was 'at all secure' because in his view 'The Ofsted inspection process is unscientific' (quoted in Macleod 2004b). The value of the stakeholder satisfaction surveys used by Matthews and Sammons to inform their analysis and the rigour of Ofsted inspection methodology are linked issues because it seems likely that in expressing satisfaction about Ofsted, practitioners and other stakeholders are often giving too much credibility to its inspection methodology. Yet as noted in Chapter 2, academic assessments of Ofsted methodology have long been scathing and they have not disappeared as indicated by the calls for a Royal Commission. So why in all the debate around Ofsted is there not wider interest in the rigour of its evidence? A key issue is likely to be that whether or not Ofsted is actually getting its facts right is widely regarded as less important than the climate of accountability which it brings to bear on schools. Despite the improvements noted below, Ofsted continues to be primarily legitimated by the power of the state rather than meeting the requirements of social science.

Is Ofsted becoming more progressive?

(1) Acknowledgement of contextual constraints

Ofsted's perspective on context, as reflected in the annual reports of the Chief Inspector and in various speeches, certainly indicates an improved recognition of contextual constraints on schools. Most obviously the 2002 annual report of Chief Inspector David Bell acknowledged that 'There remain some groups of pupils and some schools for whom raising standards remains an almost intractable challenge' (Ofsted 2003b; see also Curtis 2003a). This is not the kind of thing Chris Woodhead would have ever admitted. In a speech to the Fabian Society, Bell (2003a) also noted:

- That since 1996, the socio-economic attainment gap has narrowed in primary schools but it has widened somewhat in secondary schools.
- That low SES schools are marked by disconnection, recruitment problems and high turnover of pupils and that 'Where factors like these are present, and compound one another, schools are fragile places.'
- The need for 'caution against unrealistic expectations about how quickly deep change can be effected', there being 'no new magic recipe' for dealing with low attaining schools. 'The brutal fact of the matter is that the difficulties that some schools face have been around for many years and successive governments, national and local, have not conclusively dealt with them.'
- 'That there is absolutely no place for demonizing those schools and those – adults and children – who work in them. This is not about a "blame culture", castigating insensitively those who are tackling formidable challenges with resolution and commitment.'

Putting some of this thinking into practice, Ofsted's instruction to lead inspectors post-September 2003 has been to shape inspection to reflect the main features of schools (Ofsted 2003c). There has been an increased emphasis on context in the 2003 school Performance and Assessment Reports (PANDAs)[4] with inspectors now also advised not to use the PANDA data inflexibly but rather to 'consider the PANDA report in the light of school's circumstances, drawing on other available information as appropriate' (Ofsted 2004a: 2). Similarly there is new recognition in the inspection framework introduced in September 2003 that free school meals (FSMs) may not be a fair reflection of social context and that inspectors should use their discretion (Ofsted 2003b: 39) as well as new emphasis on 'the effect of any particular aids or barriers to raising achievement, either within the school or externally' (Ofsted 2003b: 127). These are significant developments and may be seen as a far cry from the days when Woodhead refused to adopt a stronger contextual indicator on the grounds that 'it is essential that Ofsted does nothing to encourage the use of pupils' backgrounds as an excuse for poor performance' (Woodhead letter to the TES, 1 March 1996).

There nevertheless remain important limits to the extent to which Ofsted is willing to recognize structural constraints. For instance, in response to research by Ruth Lupton which illustrated that most schools in special measures were in deprived areas and questioned whether Ofsted inspections took account of the depressing effect of poverty on the effectiveness of school processes (e.g. see Lupton 2004, also Chapter 6), an Ofsted spokesperson stated:

> Deprivation must not be an excuse for unsatisfactory provision. Subsequent reports on schools that have been through special measures show just what can be done even in the most difficult circumstances. ('Does Ofsted ignore effects of poverty?' 2002)

Similarly, despite its concern with context, Bell's Fabian speech notes 'no room for an "excuse culture"' which he describes as a 'patronizing or indulgent approach which condones low expectations or overstates the intractability of the external pressures'. It also illustrates the continuing importance of 'exemplary schools' in Ofsted thinking:

> '[There are] higher-attaining disadvantaged urban schools which are better led and managed and more effective. ... Explanation of the success of these schools is well documented by Ofsted and others. Essentially what makes the difference, as our publication "Improving City Schools" said a couple of years ago, is "the clarity, intensity and persistence of the schools' work and the rigour with which it is scrutinized. At best, all the energy of the school serves the same end, raising standards".' (Bell 2003a)

(2) Market forces and privatization

Ofsted has at times provided evidence and arguments against the extension of markets and private sector involvement in education. An argument in Bell's Fabian speech may be seen as unexceptional given the extent of New Labour intervention in education, nevertheless it does recognize that a purely market-based approach to the provision of schooling would not work:

> 'I think it is naive in the extreme to think that dramatic change will be brought about in every school if only structures or governance

are changed. Do those who advocate unrestrained competition between schools, with no kind of regulation or oversight, really believe that the public good would be better served? Frankly, I doubt it.' (Bell 2003a)

Ofsted inspections have also highlighted problems with the privatization of LEAs. Under gradings introduced by Ofsted in December 2002, five of the nine LEAs with privatized services were rated as poor improvers (Southwark, Swindon, Walsall, Waltham Forest and Hackney), three (Bradford, Haringey and Islington) were rated unsatisfactory and just one (Leeds) was rated satisfactory (Slater 2003a). On the other hand, Ofsted is still very much implicated in the marketization and privatization of education. It continues to be positioned by ministers as a provider of information to inform parental choice:

> As the education inspectorate, Ofsted, said, schools would be inspected twice as often as they had in the past, the Schools Standards minister, David Miliband, said parents would get clearer information in a prospectus-style profile. ... The interval at which schools are inspected will be halved from a maximum of six years to three, so parents get more up-to-date information on their quality. (Macleod 2004a)

Ofsted inspections are also themselves contracted out and in this respect it has been a major contributor to the growth of a private market for providing educational services. This process continues in New Labour's second term with Ofsted consulting in 2002 on plans to deal with as few as eight big inspection providers instead of the previous 67, giving these eight contracts worth £45 million each. The response by support services company Capita was to immediately join up with four other providers to set up a large inspection firm (White 2002; Shaw 2002c). Here we can see Ofsted encouraging the corporatization as well as the privatization of education.

(3) Managerialism

One important theme of New Labour's second term is to try to reduce the administrative burden on schools associated with managerialism and there has been considerable attention to trying to reduce the load of Ofsted inspections. These include the announcement in June 2004 of so-called 'lighter touch' inspections and the annual report by governors to parents and the yearly meeting they are by law supposed to hold being replaced with a shorter school profile. Special measures schools are also no longer being required to produce a completely fresh action plan as Ofsted will accept a revised version of existing plans. Thus Macleod (2004a) suggests that Ofsted appears to have acknowledged what many headteachers have long complained of – that aspects of the existing system were 'unnecessarily bureaucratic and time-consuming'. There has also been a genuine reduction in the Ofsted paperwork sent out to schools (Slater 2004e). Of further interest in this area are Ofsted's recent criticisms of what Curtis (2004a) refers to as the 'primary superhead scheme' whereby primary strategy consultant leaders from more successful schools have been trained to act as consultants in a quarter of all lower achieving schools.

Despite these developments it is questionable whether a significant reduction of the administrative burden of inspections is going to be achieved because Ofsted, probably as a response to ministerial demands, is sometimes requiring a heavier load. For instance, the idea of proportionality – inspecting some schools more than others depending on how successful they are – has been seen as reducing the burden of inspections but following this model, unsuccessful schools have a considerable burden to contend with. Meanwhile there are shifts in the demands on all schools as the new 'laser' inspections are intended to be lighter. But they are more frequent too, every three years rather than every six.

As suggested by Bell's Fabian speech noted earlier, Ofsted also still emphasizes effective management as the solution to problems of educational quality and its post-September 2003 inspections look at the governance of schools, the quality of leadership and the effectiveness of management, grading each on a 1–7 scale and then averaging to create an overall leadership and management grade. To Ofsted 'The inspection framework makes much clearer distinctions between leadership at all levels, management at all levels and governance, where judgements are more clearly linked to the statutory responsibilities of the governing body and the way it supports and challenges the school' (Ofsted 2003a: 5). Yet this has also raised the stakes for heads as it requires a good score in all three categories for them to come out looking good.

Ofsted has also continued to criticize the quality of management in schools in ways which indicate management is seen as the main determinant of school quality. Thus the Primary Strategy consultant scheme was actually introduced in 2003 after Ofsted blamed weak headteachers for low results in literacy and numeracy in 2002. In an interesting twist on the costs of managerialism, poor management is seen by Ofsted to damage children's education because it means schools do not reduce the administrative burden on teachers and provide them with the guaranteed time for planning, preparation, and marking promised by ministers. Poor head teachers are also thought to fail to monitor their staff's workload, putting them at risk of becoming overburdened (Slater 2003b; Ofsted 2003d).

(4) Performativity

There have been a number of ways in which Ofsted appears to have recognized that its inspections put inappropriate pressures on teacher and heads, as well as the cost of targets for schools and students. For instance, in 2001 Tomlinson admitted that Ofsted inspections had often been damaging to the professionalism of teachers:

> There were inspectors – I put it in the past tense – and there were cases where I think that staff in schools were not treated in the way they should have been. I'm quite certain of that. I've been to schools and listened to teachers and listened to governors and I'm quite convinced from their accounts that in those instances they were not treated as professionals. (quoted in Woodward 2001)

It could be argued that Ofsted has sought to reduce pressure on schools by providing pre-inspection commentary since September 2001 which has allowed schools to respond to particular Ofsted concerns rather than trying to cover all the bases. There is also more emphasis on self-evaluation through the Form S4 provided to Ofsted teams before they arrive at schools. Proportionality may be seen to reduce inappropriate performative pressure on many schools. And by removing time for schools to respond because they only have a few days notice, the new laser inspections can be seen to reduce the fabrication associated with inspections.

Bell argued in his 2001–2002 annual report (Ofsted 2003b) that primary schools' focus on achieving government targets in English and maths was distracting them from other subjects. His 2003 York speech was highly critical of excessive use of targets:

> 'one of the things inspectors find is that an excessive or myopic focus on targets can actually narrow and reduce achievement by crowding out some of the essentials of effective and broadly-based learning. They also find teachers, heads and local authorities for whom targets are now operating more as a threat than a motivator, more as stick than carrot. Moreover, the harder the targets become, the more tempting it is to treat them with cynicism or defeatism. I have a very real concern that the innovation and reform that we need to see in our schools may be inhibited by an over-concentration on targets.' (Bell 2003b)

In the same speech there was recognition of the problem of test scores plateauing and an apparent desire to listen more to heads:

> 'the time is now right to take greater account of what headteachers are saying about the pupils in their own schools and, more specifically, what strategies they will deploy to improve attainment. We may find that schools' targets do not aggregate up to the LEA targets but this may be no bad thing if it presents a more realistic picture of expected progress.' (Bell 2003b)

What is being covered in school inspections is also changing over time and in some cases may be taking on more of a social justice agenda. For instance the post-September 2003 inspections have a greater emphasis on inclusion:

> Inclusion is more clearly signalled as a central feature of a school's effectiveness. The inspection team will focus on all aspects of inclusion, but especially race equality, special educational needs, and equality of opportunity for all groups in the school, taking particular account of their achievements. (Ofsted 2003a)

It is also possible, however, to take a more pessimistic reading of most of the above developments. To begin with, self-evaluation can simply represent the internalizing of performance requirements if it is only done to an external agenda. Moreover while more account is taken of the school's self-evaluation through Form S4, self-evaluation has proved a two-edge sword. Bangs (2004) noted that the National Union of Teachers (NUT) welcomed the new self-evaluation part of the inspection framework because it appeared to mirror the NUT's own model for school self-evaluation. However the NUT then began to get reports from schools that inspectors appeared to be highlighting the 'weaknesses' honestly identified by schools while downplaying their 'strengths'.

Proportionality also clearly represents a performative two-edge sword – it reduces the surveillance of 'successful ' schools only at the expense of increasing it in 'unsuccessful' ones and there is the highly questionable assumption that increased inspection pressure will lead to improvements in such schools.[5]

Rather than reducing fabrication, because of the implications of getting a bad Ofsted, the new short-notice 'laser' inspections will probably put schools under pressure throughout the period that a inspection could fall due. This is going to be a lot more of the time given that the new inspections are going to be every three years rather than every six. As Bangs (quoted in Macleod 2004a) has put it:

> The high stakes nature of inspections has not changed. There are many teachers who will find the prospect of reducing the agonizing run up to inspections attractive. That is understandable, but the reality is that in the year their school is to be inspected, the anticipation will dominate thinking from the beginning of the year 'till the inspection takes place. This is no way to ensure the inspection is supportive. Instead it is likely to demotivate teachers.

To Wragg (2004), 'Schools will simply be in permanent terror of the knock at the door, instead of suffering for a few weeks.'

Shaw (2003f) has noted that while the inspections introduced post-September 2003 were supposed to be 'lighter touch', they were also supposed to be more rigorous. In practice there seems little doubt that the new inspection regime became tougher as 'satisfactory' became unsatisfactory and whereas previously 20 per cent of lessons had to be unsatisfactory to trigger special measures, the proportion was halved to 10 per cent. As noted earlier, there was a rise in the rate of schools going into special measures (Curtis 2004b; Smithers 2004; Ofsted 2004b) and accusations from teacher unions of Ofsted moving the goalposts while Ofsted insisted, until insistence was no longer enough, that it was just maintaining standards.

Finally it would be wrong to read Ofsted criticisms of targets as a criticism of target setting *per se*. To Bell (2003b) it was:

'absolutely right that ambitious targets were set in areas such as attainment at 11 and 16. We were not doing well enough and we had to do better. National targets helped us to focus and especially where they were supported by significant investment in staff development and other materials, then they brought about a momentum for change. This in turn has brought about improvements in pupils' performance and teachers' skills. ... The trend over the past five years has demonstrated that having ambitious national and local targets can make a real difference and reduce dramatically the numbers failing to reach a national expectation.'

(5) Curriculum prescription

In the case of Summerhill, a legal challenge by the school forced Ofsted to recognize a different kind of curriculum than that taught in regular schools (see Chapter 5). This could be seen to have 'broken the mould' such that other schools could begin to develop more innovative curricula, particularly with the new freedoms in primary schools offered by *Excellence and Enjoyment*. In practice however, it seems that Ofsted inspections will continue to have a dampening, conservatizing effect on curriculum developments. Writing on this theme, Laar (2004) has suggested that *Excellence and Enjoyment*:

came with an unequivocal message: 'Literacy and numeracy remain vital, but we want all schools to offer pupils a rich and exciting curriculum in which all subjects are taught well.' This was backed by a promise of significant financial and practical support. Pessimistic or timorous professionals were assured that Ofsted would be part of the grand design, focusing on the extent to which schools provided a broad range of worthwhile curricular opportunities. The primary strategy offered a sense of release for primary schools, many of whom were genuinely oppressed by what they felt was relentless pressure to achieve unrealistic targets and the fear that Ofsted judgements were largely determined by SATs outcomes.

However, analysing 15 post-September 2003 reports, Laar found that core subjects were rigorously inspected but many of the foundation subjects received little more than cursory attention. While the framework

> does encourage the reporting of outstanding practice in any subject, and schools are able, through self-evaluation, to bias the process towards the foundation subjects ... it seems unlikely that this is happening. Inspection of English, maths, ICT and science continues to dominate the process at the expense of history, music and PE.

Figures from Ofsted released in July 2004 confirm the problem. Inspectors made judgements on geography or design and technology in fewer than half of schools and music was judged in only half of schools visited since the new inspection framework began last September.

Laar suggests the causes may be, variously, a significantly reduced allocation of inspection days, some subjects not being able to be timetabled during the inspection, or the inspectors being hesitant to sample complex subject areas even where the pre-inspection data suggests a major focus could be on foundation subjects. But the net effect is likely to be that '[t]he likelihood of children experiencing a rich and transforming curriculum will be diminished' (Laar 2004).

Is Ofsted becoming more progressive? Summing up

It is clear that Ofsted continues to be highly problematic from a social justice point of view. Certainly there is more acknowledgement of context and there is, as Matthews and Sammons (2004) have put it, 'a general desire to reduce unnecessary stress and workload for teachers, particularly in primary schools'. But Ofsted can do neither of these to any great extent without compromising its key role in policing market and managerial reform. In this respect it is interesting to note Ofsted's higher trust developments (such as Tomlinson's inspection only every ten years) being apparently undone by ministerial intervention. Meanwhile although Ofsted has increasingly used its 'independent' role to criticize government policy, it has also continued to do a lot of what has become more usually expected of it, for instance talking down local authorities (Clancy 2002), criticizing the standard of reading (Ward 2002), criticizing teachers' report writing ('Are your reports bland and useless?' 2003), teachers' poor English and maths knowledge (Slater 2003c) and ineffective school leaders (Slater 2003a). Ofsted is also still pulled out by New Labour to publicly wave a stick on occasion, for instance the recent announcement of snap nursery inspections after a TV documentary exposed serious concerns about the treatment of children by some carers (Hayes 2004).

What we are seeing then is some improvement but no fundamental shift. How then to explain why practitioners and the media seem to perceive a real improvement? Wragg (2004) suggests that our expectations of new inspection developments are likely to be conditioned by our experience of Ofsted up till now:

> 'Ah, but many people have said that they favour the proposed new procedures', comes the response. Of course they do, because they compare them with the old procedures, not with some paragon ideal. Tell people they are all going to be shot at dawn and no doubt three quarters would rejoice when this was commuted to amputating their left leg instead.

Certainly, what was unacceptable among educators and others yesterday is often less so today because of ideological shifts over time associated with wider neo-liberal reform. Another factor is undoubtedly the personalities involved, although this should not be disconnected from the political climate in which key actors are appointed. Tomlinson and Bell are far more empathetic to teachers than Woodhead's persona was, but then they have needed to be too.

A pessimistic picture?

It might be suggested that by selecting the two areas I have, I am painting an unduly pessimistic picture of recent changes in OSI. In fact the opposite is more likely to be true because the Primary Strategy and Ofsted are seen as areas where developments represent a more progressive educational agenda for New Labour. If these remain problematic, what does this say about the rest of OSI? The *Five Year Strategy for Children and Learners* (DfES 2004b) is also signalling more 'diversity', 'choice' and privatization as the broad direction of education policy until 2009. What is certainly not being discussed is the removal of any of the existing planks of OSI – choice and competition, local management of schools, Ofsted inspections, target setting or performance management.

This chapter has illustrated that although there may be recent shifts in OSI, they are not fundamental enough to make working with it a viable approach for those seeking serious change. This reinforces the argument for practitioners contesting rather than supporting OSI. Yet writers like Hatcher, Wright and Bottery have argued that many practitioners are unwilling to dwell on OSI's limitations, preferring to work with it in a relatively unquestioning kind of way. This issue is considered in the next chapter.

4 Even the trees are on her side

'We must go as quickly as we can,' said Mr Tumnus. 'The whole wood is full of *her* spies. Even some of the trees are on her side.' (from *The Lion, the Witch and the Wardrobe* by C.S. Lewis)

This chapter discusses issues which help to link the concerns of the preceding chapters on OSI policy with the next on the contestation of OSI. I begin by looking at the National College for School Leadership (NCSL) which claims to 'service the needs of school leaders across [the] whole country' (Newton 2001: 11), to 'avoid a narrow focus' (Southworth 2004: 341) and to be 'a focus for national and international debate on school leadership issues' (Blunkett 2000a). This all implies the NCSL has some autonomy from OSI and it is noteworthy that headteachers' associations have been reported to be 'upbeat about the NCSL's contribution' (Revell 2004). However after exploring the NCSL's website I will argue that it actually has little autonomy and is much more part of the OSI problem than a solution.

This in turn raises another question to be considered in this chapter, whether most heads and teachers are concerned to contest OSI or whether they would prefer to comply. I look at some recent academic discussion of this issue, considering headteachers separately from classroom teachers in recognition of the growing gap between them noted in Chapter 2. On balance the literature comes down on the side of teachers and heads complying with reform but I will argue that it also raises methodological issues because little of the literature engages closely with the perspectives and activities of practitioners under OSI. The scope of this discussion is another relevant issue because there are important forms of contestation, such as those involving teacher unions or professional associations, which the literature around practitioner resistance/compliance with reform rarely covers.

The NCSL: working for headteachers?[1]

The NCSL was set up in November 2000 and has grown rapidly. It now runs some 24 different kinds of school leadership programmes and funding for it from the DfES has increased from £29.2m in 2001–2002 to £111.3m in 2004–2005. In its short life it has become seen, in Tony Bush's words as 'a major influence, arguably *the* major influence, on school leadership, management and administration in England and beyond' (Bush 2004: 243).

Given its importance, there has been surprisingly little academic work about (rather than for) the NCSL. The most substantial body of work to date is in a 2004 special issue of the journal *Educational Management, Administration and Leadership*. Here there are contributions which trace the historical development of the NCSL, look at its international role, consider its organizational features and its likely impact. They are all useful in one way or another but have a mutual tendency to view the NCSL as a largely beneficial development. This may be because none of the contributors tap into very critical perspectives either within or beyond the education management arena. As is too often the case in the education management and leadership arena, contributors with more critical outlooks needed to be sought. Another likely problem is that as the NCSL has become more influential, many in the school leadership and management arena have carried out work for it, including funded research and consultancy. Indeed Weindling (2004) has shown that by 2002 the NCSL was funding nearly 50 per cent of the UK research on education leadership. Since a number of the contributors to the *EMAL* collection are strongly linked to the NCSL, the rather benign picture of the NCSL they paint may have partly resulted from 'buy in'. To his credit, this is a problem recognized by the editor of the collection, Tony Bush, who notes that his wide involvement in the NCSL 'means that it is difficult to remain objective' (Bush 2004: 243).

Nevertheless if the reader is prepared to dwell on various issues mentioned in passing, the *EMAL* contributions do signal possibilities for a more fundamental critique of the NCSL. Some of the issues raised by the *EMAL* contributions include:

- While the NCSL does not claim a monopoly on excellence, the government has decided it should provide a single national focus for school leadership development and research. Bush (p. 245) suggests this is 'ambitious, probably not wise and manifestly untrue' but notes the NCSL does have a near monopoly over the training of aspiring heads who from April 2004 must have the National Professional Qualification for Headship (NPQH) or be enrolled on it before they can take up headteacher posts.
- The NPQH 'provides a worthwhile starting point for a system that previously had no minimum requirements for headship but it is below the intellectual level regarded as necessary by several other countries' (Bush, p. 246).
- Leadership constructs like 'transformational leadership' which often start out as descriptive and explanatory research tools become translated into prescriptive theories designed to encourage particular types which are incorporated in leadership development programmes (Bolam 2004: 258). To Bolam 'there is nothing wrong in principle with this. ... But the strengths and weaknesses of their evidential base should be made clear.'
- The NCSL regards closeness to policy as an advantage. Walker and Dimmock (2004: 273) cite an NCSL report which argues that 'One strength of NCSL, which almost none of the other centres [for leadership development have], is the potential closeness to government and therefore the opportunity to influence policy and practice' (NCSL 2002: 1).
- As a fledgling organization, 'enormous' political pressures were placed on the NCSL to meet various government requirements, e.g. Ofsted wanted the NCSL to explore the implications of its inspection data-base (Mulford 2004: 315–16).
- In the early days of the NCSL there was an unwillingness to engage with academics (Mulford, p. 316).
- Participants in early seminars run by the NCSL came away recognizing that much of the agenda had been decided (Mulford, p. 316).

- The NCSL has been reluctant to publish any critically constructive material (Mulford, p. 318).
- There are continuing problems with the quality of the NCSL's research (Mulford, p. 320).
- School leaders surveyed in 2001 felt that the NCSL 'needed to show its independence and demonstrate that it was not simply another arm of government, or more specifically, of the DfES (Earley and Evans 2004: 336).

These points obliquely and more directly signal the relevance of an analysis developed by Gronn 2003 who argues that bodies like the NCSL are engaged in a process of 'designer leadership' by accrediting school leaders according to managerialist national standards. Expanding on Gronn, who focuses mostly on the role of national standards, the argument here will be that the wider thrust of the NCSL is also to frame up school leadership so as to uncritically relay managerialist education policy into schools. I discuss designer leadership in more detail and consider the NCSL's wider framing up of school leadership by way of a trawl through its website. I also note some developments signalled in the recent 'End to End' review of the NCSL (Review Team 2004) which are likely to bring this body even more into line with OSI than it already is.

Designer leadership and the NCSL

Gronn writes about designer leadership in his recent book *The New Work of Educational Leaders* (Gronn 2003). By designer leadership he means the use of mandatory standards of assessment and accreditation for school leaders. He argues that designer leadership represents a distinctive break from previous ascriptive and credentialist approaches to leadership formation by requiring the customization of leadership programmes to fit national or system-wide standards of effective leadership. If ascriptive leadership was about naturally fitted leaders and credentialist leadership about formally fitted leaders, designer leadership is about suitably fitted leaders, i.e. it involves much more control over what kind of school leader it is possible to be.

Gronn links designer leadership to the New Public Management and the use of national standards by governments to regulate education from a distance. To Gronn, such standards are the vehicles for the steerers of systems to micromanage the day-to-day work of school leaders. In England the TTA released National Standards for Headteachers in 1997 and these formed the basis for three leadership development programmes which it developed and which were then subsequently taken over by the NCSL: the National Professional Qualification for Headteachers (NPQH) for aspiring heads, the Headteacher Leadership and Management Programme (HEADLAMP) for newly appointed heads (now replaced by HIP the Headteacher Induction Programme), and the Leadership Programme for Serving Headteachers (LPSH) for heads who have been in post for a while.

Gronn points to many significant problems with leadership standards and the leadership programmes which stem from them. First, the leadership standards emphasize an ideal of 'hero' or 'superhead' transformational leadership rather than shared leadership whereas schools, he argues, should be seen as communities of practice. There has been recent interest in 'distributed leadership' by the NCSL but then this is a notion easily colonized and stripped of progressive intent (Thrupp 2004). Second, like performative measures in other areas, standards are altering career incentives, rewards and mobility. Heads are becoming necessarily concerned with accreditation in conformity with standards rather than really interrogating the value of what they are being taught. Third, he suggests standards-based leadership programmes are likely to narrow the range of kinds of people becoming heads and that when faced with numerous candidates taking the same 'line' on leadership, selection panels may choose heads for inappropriate reasons. Finally, and most importantly, since standards are intended to eliminate variation and de-legitimate context, they tend to be generic and normative rather than evidence-based. Since they do not have to fit with the situated realities of leadership they are open to predation by the demands of managerialism (if in doubt put it in a standard) and they also set up a compliance culture which fits neatly with managerialism. Gronn concludes:

> In a political climate conducive to greater regulation and the decreased autonomy of the professions, standards are increasingly being used to do the work of regulating the members of key occupational groups. Standards for the preparation and development of school leaders represent the principal instrument by which public authorities are customising their needs ... a machinery of preferred outcome statements drives judgements about proficiency and levels of performance. Unlike previous arrangements governed by ascriptive and achievement norms, little is left to chance in customized approaches to leader-making. (Gronn 2003: 24)

While Gronn's arguments about designer leadership are persuasive they also present problems when used to understand the NCSL. First, while generic National Standards remain very much in place (revised National Standards for Headteachers were published in September 2004), and while some NCSL web pages note that NCSL programmes are underpinned by these National Standards, assessing the extent to which this is really the case for particular programmes would require careful analysis of on-line and other course materials including those used in residentials. These are generally only available to those taking the programmes with the on-line elements (i.e. the Learning Gateway which incorporates talk2learn) being password protected. But in any case it is apparent that the NCSL is doing much more than providing school leadership programmes. It is also more broadly framing up school leadership through research, publications and other services for school leaders provided through its website and at organized events.

The NCSL's wider framing of school leadership

Since the NCSL website is at the centre of its communications with school leaders, here I use parts of it (basically the open parts as even some areas outside its actual programmes are password protected) to explore the NCSL's general approach to school leadership. I am particularly concerned to explore the extent to which it is simply relaying OSI policy or whether there is any sign of it exposing school leaders to debate about that policy in a way that would indicate some independence from the DfES and other central agencies. Some observations then – starting with the main links on the home page www.ncsl.org.uk, as it was presented in November 2004.

On the left of the NCSL homepage are some of its more permanent links:

- updates
- managing your school
- leadership development
- the knowledge pool
- research & development
- national remodelling team
- networked learning
- community leadership
- LEArning with LEAs
- online communities
- the college
- NCSL quick links – these include the A–Z of School Leadership, essential documents, example policies, Headlamp, HIP (Headteacher Induction Programme), Leadership Development Framework, Leadership Links, Leading from the Middle, LPSH, NCSL programmes, Networked Learning Communities, NPQH, and the Matrix
- Other sites – these include BBC learning, BBC news, BECTA (British Educational Communications and Technology Agency), British Council, DfES news, Fast Track Teaching, GovernorNet, GTC (General Teaching Council), Guardian Education, Hands on Support diagnostic tool, NgfL (National grid for Learning), Ofsted, QCA (Qualifications and Curriculum Authority), Teacher Net, TES, and the TTA (Teacher Training Agency).

In the centre of the page are 'log in' buttons for the 'Learning Gateway' and 'talk2learn' as well as 'Community news' (e.g., join a debate about the Tomlinson report) There is also BBC news for education (recent media coverage) and NCSL news, e.g.:

- Tomlinson report now available: download the report
- Leading from the Middle: apply now online

- Distributed leadership: book for the launch on 29 November
- Conference 2005: online registration now available
- New Heads Conference 2004: register online
- CSBM: application round open.

On the right of the page are links to LEAs, links to NCSL in the regions (various affiliated centres) and reminder for school leaders (e.g. NPQH application round opens). There are also recent publications as below (with the sponsoring agency in brackets):

- A National Conversation about Personalised Learning (DfES)
- National Standards for Headteachers (DfES – TeacherNet)
- Pupil Achievement Tracker (DfES)
- Stats4schools: lesson plans and data sets (Office for National Statistics)
- Spectrum 78 (DfES – TeacherNet)
- Five-year strategy for children and learners (DfES)
- Learning about personalisation by Charles Leadbeater (Demos)
- A new relationship with schools – proposals for the future of inspection (Ofsted)
- Capital funding for joint school and college ventures (DfES – TeacherNet)
- Evaluation of Key Stage 3 strategy: third year (Ofsted)
- Schools' financial benchmarking website (DfES – TeacherNet)
- Every Child Matters green paper (DfES)
- Leadership and Management: What inspection tells us (Ofsted).

Even without going more deeply into the website, a strong relationship between the NCSL and the other education agencies is apparent from the 'other sites', 'recent publications' and LEA links on the homepage. Going into the links (all those not password protected) does little to dispel this first impression, for instance:

Education updates. Under this heading are a long list of DfES consultations, the BBC news for education and 'a filtered list of publications that have particular relevance to school leaders'. This list of publications from the last two years is dominated by the monthly issues of Spectrum, a DfES digest of 'news and publications of interest to schools'. Those aside, other publications (with source in brackets) are:

2004
June – Euro 2004: what could you be doing in school? (DfES – TeacherNet), ICT in schools: the impact of government initiatives five years on (Ofsted)
May – NFER News, Spring 2004 (NFER), School in Focus – celebrating success in schools (DfES – TeacherNet)
April – Creating a school website (DfES-TeacherNet)
February – ICT performance indicator results (BECTA)
January – 14–19 Pathfinders: an evaluation of the first year (DfES)

2003
October – Survey of ICT in schools (DfES)
September – Governing body procedures from 1 September 2003 (DfES – TeacherNet)
September – Statutory guidance on the school governance procedures (DfES – TeacherNet)
September – Cutting burdens (DfES – TeacherNet)
July – Leadership and Management: what inspection tells us (Ofsted)
May – Fulfilling the potential – transforming teaching and learning through ICT in schools (NCSL)
March – Information Management Strategy (DfES)
February – Teachers' pay 2003 Documents and explanatory notes (DfES – TeacherNet)
February – Annual Report of Her Majesty's Chief Inspector of Schools Standards and Quality in Education 2001/02 (Ofsted)
January – 14–19 Opportunity and Excellence (DfES)

Managing your school This leads to further links: 'Policies', 'Essential documents', 'Online tools', 'National initiatives', 'Bursar development' and 'Financial management'. The first are example policies on everything the DfES or Ofsted would be likely to require of a school. The second, 'Essential documents' are actually all DfES, QCA and Ofsted policies and circulars. 'Online tools' include a link to the DfES website where there is an A–Z of school leadership which provides a guide to DfES policies for heads as well as the teachers' pay calculator from the DfES TeacherNet site. 'National initiatives' provides a list of all current initiatives and links to several in particular: the Primary Strategy Leadership Programme, Learning and Teaching using ICT, Hands on Support, The Strategic Leadership of ICT (SLICT) programme, Technical support, the Key Stage 3 National Strategy and the National Numeracy Strategy. Generally these are links to DfES or BECTA pages although the NCSL is itself involved in some of these initiatives. The 'Bursar development' link outlines the Certificate of School Business Management (CSBM). The 'Financial Management' links offer financial advice of various kinds for schools. An introduction from then Education Secretary Charles Clarke explains

> It is vital that schools can plan and manage their resources effectively to achieve the highest possible standards. I therefore asked the National College for School Leadership and KPMG [an international corporation specialising in audit, tax and business advice], working in association with headteacher and governor associations, to design and develop a varied menu of support and guidance to help schools' budget management, and create greater financial stability for them.

Most of the rest of the links on the homepage need not detain us either because they variously lead to password protected programmes ('Leadership development', 'Networked learning', 'Community leadership', 'LEArning with LEAs', 'Online communities'), or are evidently DfES connected ('National Remodelling team', 'LEArning with LEAs'), or they repeat the same links (for instance the first few 'quick links' are the same – 'Policies', 'Essential documents' and 'Leadership A–Z' as in 'Managing your school' above, the remainder being NCSL leadership programmes). But the 'Knowledge pool' is of particular interest because it seems the most likely area to demonstrate some independence from New

Labour education policy. There are three parts to it: 'Foundations', 'Leadership links' and 'Key reads'.

'Foundations' contains the 'Leadership Evidence Base' where 'a number of key people nationally and from around the world were invited to write short essays drawing upon thinking on effective school leadership. The essays acted as a launch pad for building the College's research role'. Here they are, arranged by author:

- Andy Hargreaves and Dean Fink: Educational reform and school leadership in 3-D perspective.
- Barbara MacGilchrist: Leading the intelligent school.
- Barry McGaw: Some research issues for the National College for School Leadership.
- Brent Davies: From school development plans to a strategic planning framework.
- Brian Caldwell: Leadership and innovation in the transformation of schools.
- Bruce Barnett: Changing external policy context and the role of the school principal.
- Christopher Day and Alma Harris: Effective school leadership.
- David Bennett: School of the future: key issues for school leaders.
- David Hopkins: Instructional leadership and school improvement.
- David Istance: Work on schooling for tomorrow: trends, themes and scenarios to inform leadership issues.
- David Reynolds: Effective school leadership: the contributions of school effectiveness research.
- Geoff Southworth: Leading learning and teaching primary schools.
- Howard Green: Ten questions for school leaders.
- John MacBeath: Leadership: learning to live with contradiction.
- John West-Burnham: Learning to lead.
- Kate Myers: Leadership in action – talking heads: prepare to be surprised.

- Kenneth Leithwood: Educational accountability and school leadership.
- Louise Stoll: Enhancing internal capacity: leadership for learning.
- Marc Tucker and Judy Codding: School headship in the United States: a situation report.
- Mel Ainscow: Developing inclusive schools: implications for leadership.
- Michael Barber: High expectations and standards for all, no matter what: the leadership challenge for a world-class education service.
- Michael Fullan: Role of the head in school improvement.
- Ofsted: Leadership in schools.
- Patricia Collarbone: Reflections on headship: grounded leadership – lessons from the field.
- Peter Hill: What headteachers need to know about teaching and learning.
- Tim Brighouse: Passionate leadership.
- Vicki Phillips: Leadership in education: flavour of the month or serious business?

Many of the authors here are those I have criticized for textual apologism as part of my discussions of school effectiveness and education management over recent years (Thrupp 1999; Thrupp and Willmott 2003). Indeed the list includes many of those whose work provided extended case studies of subtle or overt apologism (e.g. Barber, Davies, Fullan, Hopkins, Stoll, Southworth), while the work of Caldwell has been widely criticized for its simplistic support for neo-liberal reform (e.g. Smyth 1993). Conversely there is no-one here known for critical perspectives on leadership, e.g. Blackmore (Blackmore 1999), Gewirtz (Gewirtz 2002), Grace (Grace 1995) Gunter (Gunter 2001) Ozga (Ozga and Walker 1995) or Smyth (Smyth 1989). My point is not that any of those who wrote essays should not have been invited to do so but that there is an obvious but unacknowledged politics to the work selected. Also on the 'Foundations' page is a link to Hay McBer's 'Models of Excellence for School Leaders'. Like their better-known work on teacher competencies (Hay McBer 2000), this material is extremely technicist.

The second link within the Knowledge Pool is 'Key Reads'. Until December 2004 this link provided a set of references with a very similar flavour to the 'Leadership Evidence Base' noted above; for instance, these were the 'Leadership' references:

Caldwell, B. J. and Spinks, J. M. (1992) *Leading the Self-Managing School*.

Caldwell, B. J. and Spinks, J. M. (1998) *Beyond the Self-Managing School*.

Davies, B. and Ellison, L. (1997) *School Leadership for the 21st Century*.

Day, C., Harris, A., Hadfield, M., Tolley, H. and Beresford, J. (2000) *Leading Schools in Times of Change*.

Fullan, M. (2001) *Leading In a Culture of Change*.

Fullan, M. (ed.) (2000) *The Jossey-Bass Reader on Educational Leadership*.

Fullan, M. (1998) *Leadership for the 21st Century: Breaking the Bonds of Dependency*.

Jackson, D. (2000) *School Improvement and the Planned Growth of Leadership Capacity*.

Lambert, L. (1998) *Building Leadership Capacity in Schools*.

Macbeath, J. and Myers, K. (1999) *Effective School Leaders*.

Southworth, G. (1995) *Talking Heads: Voices of Experience*.

From December 2004 this link was changed to connect with *What Leaders Read*, two reviews of literature carried out for NCSL. *What Leaders Read 1: Key texts from the business world* is described on the website as 'not specifically related to education; rather they draw on the more general leadership cannon'. This review was carried out by a group from the Lancaster University Management School. *What Leaders Read 2: Key texts from education and beyond* examines 'a selection of key texts from both educational and non-educational literature in order to consider their relevance to school leaders'. This review was carried out by Mel West and colleagues at the University of Manchester. Overall there are 47 books reviewed of which only 18 have an education focus and only one, Gerald Grace's *School Leadership: Beyond Education Management* (Grace 1995) with its discussion of 'policy scholarship' versus 'policy science', comes from a clearly critical perspective.

The third link under the 'Knowledge Pool' offers 'a list of key links of interest for school leaders'. These are:

- Leadership A–Z (DfES)
- BBC
- British Council
- General Teaching Council
- National Grid for Learning
- Ofsted
- Teachernet (DfES)
- TTA
- Audit Commission
- BECTA
- DfES
- Governornet (DfES)
- National Remodelling Team
- QCA
- TES
- Webwise (BBC's beginners guide to the Internet)

While a more comprehensive and actually very good list of external links is also provided, what is of interest here is the dominance of government websites among those recommended as of 'key' interest for school leaders.

The NCSL: summing up

Much more could be said about the NCSL website and readers are encouraged to explore it themselves. But even this brief discussion illustrates that, further to Gronn's ideas about designer leadership, the NCSL is more generally being used as a conduit or relayer of New Labour policy into schools while critical perspectives which do not fit with government policy are largely ignored. National remodelling and financial advice for schools are two areas where the NCSL has quite explicitly been the delivery arm of the DfES but more generally the NCSL is promoting an approach to school leadership which is very much dominated by OSI and is drawing on academic work which is, by and large, unlikely to challenge that agenda. Since the NCSL is an arm of government this may be considered unsurprising but as noted earlier its links to OSI are not emphasized in the NCSL's official rhetoric or that of its key personnel.

If the NCSL was really a place for open debate on school leadership issues, we would expect to find critics of New Labour education policy welcomed in to give their point of view. In fact what is apparent is how tightly the discussion space is controlled. There may be room for a token dissenter – but only just![2] The problem is not just a lack of the kind of intellectual confidence that values critique. More fundamentally, exposing practitioners to a limited range of 'on message' perspectives serves to make sure practitioners are hearing only the academic voices most supportive of government policy.

Nevertheless worse may be yet to come. The recent 'end to end' review of the NCSL identified 'achieving a more productive DfES–NCSL relationship' as one of ten issues which need to be addressed over the next three years (Review Team 2004: 1). It argued:

> there is scope for the relationship between DfES and NCSL to become more productive. This would enable the agenda on school leadership to be shared more fully and would help the sincere convictions that drive NCSL and DfES to be more closely aligned, within and between them. A key feature of the relationship to date has been an increasing number of bilateral agreements between parts of the DfES and parts of NCSL. This has provided opportunities that each one values, and NCSL has responded well to Departmental requests. But this way of deploying the College's overall leadership development resource can make it hard to achieve a coherent integration of policy and practice. In future it would help both parties to have an overall 'agenda' and priorities that were more integrated and explicit between and within the two organizations. (NCSL Review Team 2004: 7)

The review went on to suggest various ways in which closer alignment with the DfES might be facilitated. While it was acknowledged that the NCSL has to 'manage the difficult balance between responding to DFES demands and also maintaining credibility with the profession', the NCSL was nevertheless expected to fall more clearly into line with the DfES Five Year Strategy for Children and Learners (DfES 2004b).

A subsequent remit letter to the NCSL from Education Secretary Ruth Kelly underlines the DfES's concern to tighten its grip on the NCSL (Kelly 2004). There is to be a new NCSL 'gatekeeper' unit at the DfES to keep more control over the focus of the NCSL and a stepped-up pattern of weekly and monthly meetings between NCSL and DfES officials and termly meetings ('stocktakes') between the NCSL council and senior executive and ministers.

All in all it seems likely that the NCSL will be more strongly controlled by the DfES in the future and the latest remit letter has drawn some unfavourable media comment because of this ('Ministerial diktat will stifle heads' (2005)). Nevertheless the NCSL is already deeply problematic because of its existing links to the DfES and other education agencies. The latest developments will merely intensify an existing problem.

'Mediating' headteachers: a case of wishful thinking?

In this section I consider recent arguments for and against headteachers as practitioners who are responding critically or selectively to OSI in important ways. While some have written optimistically about headteachers' ability to 'mediate' policy, there is no doubt heads are also the practitioners most worked upon by New Labour – the target of most of the NCSL programmes, involved in networks set up by central and local government, called in for seminars and meetings, the most obvious target when a school is found to be 'failing' by Ofsted and if on-message, the practitioners most often held up as examples to be emulated. As a result we could expect headteachers to be under considerable pressure to support OSI.

It is this problem which is emphasized in more critical accounts. Hatcher (2005) concludes that:

> given the structural role of headteachers in locking Labour's education project in place it seems unlikely that they can be

depended on as the principal agents of resistance to it. As Wright says, 'heads know that their schools have to succeed in a target-based culture and in the end this will drive what is allowed and what is proscribed' (Hatcher 2005: 260, citing Wright 2003: 142)

Moreover he argues (p. 261):

the evidence demonstrates the subordination of transformational and distributed leadership to government-driven managerialism. It can be seen as further confirmation of the limitations of the possibility of reinterpretation at school level in the education policy process which was the subject of debate ten years ago (see Ball 1993, and Hatcher and Troyna 1994), and which subsequent developments, and the work of Ball himself on cultures of performativity (e.g. Ball 2001) have tended to confirm.

Hatcher (and Wright) are responding to what they see as over-optimistic accounts of the ability of heads to avoid the effects of reform. One of these was the 'Effective Headteachers' research undertaken by Christopher Day and colleagues and written up in their book *Leading Schools in Times of Change* (Day *et al.* 2000). Recognizing the ethical tensions for English school leaders created by OSI, this study of 12 head teachers suggested that they could be seen as either 'subcontractors' or 'subversives':

As subcontractors they become one more link in a chain leading down from those who have developed a policy through its various stages of implementation until it impacts on teachers and pupils. The limit that this role places on their autonomy and decision-making, combined with the visibility and public nature of their loss of control, is likely to undermine their moral authority as leaders as they seek to justify the unjustifiable. The role of the subversive, on the other hand, may raise issues of duplicity and intrigue, which may tarnish their moral lead within the school. (p. 156)

But having identified this important tension, Day and colleagues argue that the heads they researched managed to accommodate it: 'The heads in the study were neither subcontractors nor subversives, but, with integrity *they skilfully mediated external changes* so that they integrated with the vision and values which existed in the schools' (p. 156, my emphasis).

Commenting on this study, Hatcher (2005: 259) notes:

> if, as [Day *et al.* 2000] say, 'Power and politics will continue to provide the context and daily realities for life in all schools' (p. 177) – a context of 'policy interventions and edicts that require compliance' (p. 139) – then 'effective leadership' becomes reduced to 'the management of the tensions and dilemmas which these create' and it is difficult to see much space for reinterpretation of policy, whatever the head's 'strong values framework'. (Day *et al.* 2000 p. 177)

Given its claims, we need to consider carefully the evidence base of the study by Day and colleagues. *Leading Schools in Times of Change* draws on interviews with heads, other staff, governors and students. The analyses attach much weight to headteachers' discourses of putting their educational values first, for instance:

> There is nothing more important than the pupils in the school, not the budget, not Ofsted, nothing. They are what we are here for and their wellbeing and success is of paramount importance. (Secondary head cited in Day *et al.* 2000: 156)

However the numerous quotes provided from heads indicate that they probably were going 'with' imposed policy most of the time. The most relevant section on 'subcontracting versus mediation' does not provide so much evidence of mediation in the sense of political critique and response as of struggling to incorporate constant reform into schools, for instance:

> It is difficult to plan too far ahead because 'politics' may dictate further changes. My mind runs ahead of the game ... we need to be proactive not reactive, but we have to carefully manage innovation to minimize the workload of, and impact on, the staff. (Primary head cited in Day *et al.* 2000: 154)

The most 'dissenting' quote in the book is probably as follows but to what extent the secondary head concerned was carrying out the 'not useful' policy mentioned is unclear:

> I don't mind taking decisions as long as they are sensible ones. I dislike taking decisions that are imposed from outside and that are not useful to the school. (p. 154)

In a similarly 'apolitical' way, a section of the book on 'Outwards looking in: being ahead of the game' provides an argument that heads were being 'proactive rather than reactive to external change' (p. 49) but there is nothing here to indicate a mindset of contesting policy, rather more a sense of wanting to take one's lead from it:

> Every step has to be checked before going ahead … (p. 49)

> You are looking at government papers, you're reading, talking, listening to other people. (p.59)

The section on 'monitoring' notes how heads saw it as not an entirely rational process … it was tied to targets, standards and achievement' (p. 54), but the emphasis is on the difficulties of monitoring rather than any critique of the politics of performativity.

The Day *et al.* study includes comments from other school actors and these reinforce the picture of heads being highly enthusiastic in picking up new reforms, for instance:

> He has tended in the past to respond too quickly to new initiatives (as soon as he has heard the announcements on Radio 4) – he has to learn to act when the proposed changes are more definite. (Deputy head, p. 65)

> She does things yesterday and we have to, or I have to, get her to do them tomorrow. (Deputy head, p. 155)

There is evidence of the enthusiasm of heads for entrepreneurial activities:

> He is good at pushing for things, technology status … (p. 93)

> The head has her finger on the pulse and is very good at seeing the opportunity for getting more funding. (p. 105)

Another study criticized by Hatcher and Wright for being unrealistic is the 'Principled principals' research of Peter Earley, Anne Gold and colleagues (Earley *et al.* 2002; Gold *et al.* 2003). They argue that the ten 'outstanding' school leaders they researched were 'principled principals' who accommodated the tensions between managerialism and education by 'translating their educational values into management and leadership practices' (Gold *et al.* 2003: 127):

> They were principled individuals with a strong commitment to their 'mission'. ... They endeavoured to *mediate* the many externally driven directives to ensure, as far as it was possible, that their take-up was consistent with what the school was trying to achieve. ... This is not to say that school leaders were unaware of the need to manage resources effectively, including human resources, and of the significance of parental choice and market forces, but that they were not fundamental. They were driven by a different set of values and these, as other studies of effective leaders suggest (e.g. Campbell, Gold and Lunt (forthcoming); Day *et al.* 2000) were *based on intrinsic values and not those imposed by others, including governments*. (Gold *et al.* 2003: 136, my emphasis)

Wright (2003) has argued of the 'Principled principals' study that in four respects it fails to challenge the view that heads are working to the OSI agenda (or, in his words, are exercising 'bastard leadership'[3]). First it doesn't explore the ends to which heads are working or their scope to choose alternative ends. Second, evidence of second order values such as teamwork, questioning and inclusive meetings and decision-making are not in themselves evidence that heads are not working towards the requirements of OSI. As he notes 'Organized crime, for example, surely makes good use of teamwork!' (p. 141). Third, he argues that any shift towards different values by the NCSL will be undone by the demands of Ofsted inspections. Fourth, and similarly, Wright stresses that there is not much prospect for the development of professional learning communities while a target-based culture is still in place. He concludes:

> What [Gold and colleague's] article and this reply show is that bastard leadership is a subtle capturing of the leadership discourse. Propounding second order values as evidence of principled leadership in fact offers no defence against bastard leadership. (Wright 2003: 142)

The 'Principled principals' study again drew mostly on interviews but included documentary analysis and attendance at leadership team meetings (the latter must have been very limited as the average time in each school, including interviews, was just two days). This study also provides no clear evidence of policy mediation. Echoing the research of Day and colleagues, the concern of heads seems to be how to keep up with constant reform but not necessarily how to challenge its assumptions:

> Several of the school leaders were generally proactive in their attitude to change, although for reportedly different reasons: one was good at 'environmental scanning' in order to anticipate 'what is coming along and preparing ourselves for it, so that when it does happen it's not such a shock'. Another told us if you don't do something different, you won't 'move on'. In another school a member of staff remarked that the head was 'good at saying "let's take the good bits"' but was reluctant to take up the latest government initiative (in this case that of becoming a professional development or 'beacon' school) because it was felt that one more initiative might cause them to 'take their eye off the ball'. We also heard about a school which had taken on several new initiatives where the school leader explained to us that the new initiatives 'make the school feel good about itself and give people a chance to raise their own game and learn'. (Gold *et al.* 2003: 132)

The section of the 'Principled principals' research most indicative of political dissent is probably as follows:

> Another school leader ... did not believe in change for change's sake – not all initiatives were considered to be good for the school, but all must go through a filtering process of 'a healthy disrespect for change'. A school leader of a nursery and infants school protected her staff from multiple innovations by filtering external demands to try to ensure that 'we do what we think is best for our children'. She thought that the self-confidence and assurance that had grown during her leadership tenure ensured she was not 'jumping just because someone was telling you to jump'. (Gold *et al.* 2003: 132)

Crucially we do not know how and to what extent these school leaders were willing or able to act as filters. Yet other research evidence from the UK (Gewirtz 2002; Grace 1995; Moore, George and Halpin 2002) and overseas (McInerney 2003) is not very encouraging. This is because while there is some evidence of headteachers being concerned about a shift from 'welfarism' to 'new managerialism', the shift nevertheless seems to be fairly wholesale and there is little evidence of headteachers being willing or able to move beyond critique to substantively contest reform. Australian principals in McInerney's (2003) research report discussion of 'old' and 'new' leadership and managerialism infecting their professional discourses:

> We were told by a principal that the term 'old leadership' was often applied to school leaders who still clung to social-democratic principles. Margaret related how a colleague, who missed out on a leadership position, was accused by the chair of the panel of being an 'old-fashioned' leader. 'Being old-fashioned', it was explained, 'is being too democratic and talking too much about social justice.' (p. 64)

> So much of what I hear at principals' meetings is managerialism. The jargon is business jargon. Every now and then someone reminds us all that we are here for the kids and for five minutes we will mouth platitudes about the kids and then we will go back to managerialism. [But] our business is all about relationships ... about working with kids ... about creating respect, attitudes, atmospheres with those kids that are conducive to them taking chances. (p. 67, citing a principal)

Others have noted that heads may mask their managerialist work with seemingly progressive language. The study by Moore, George and Halpin of eight headteachers notes that to achieve staff compliance some of the headteachers adopted 'essentially Taylorist forms and styles of management couched within some of the more "acceptable" language and aspects of "TQM" forms and styles' (p. 181) They give the example of a headteacher

> using her authority to coerce staff into her mode of thinking and operating within the school, and thereby implementing the cultural and structural reforms required by government at the local level. She masks this process, however, by couching it within a values-laden discourse of collegiality and 'trust' (Moore, George and Halpin 2002: 182)

In the EU study of Wyeham discussed in Chapter 2, which involved repeated interviews with six secondary heads, a particularly instructive case was that of Mr Weller who was more outspoken about contesting policy he didn't like than the heads in either of the previous studies:

> 'One of the things I do is I try and filter the agenda for the school. And I think that's one of the roles of a Head. … And what I try and do is I try and pick through what I think is nonsense, and onerous and bureaucratic, and what I think is actually – is gonna make a difference.'

> 'And in the end, you know, I don't mind breaking a few rules. You know, what are they gonna do, sack me? You know, and what are they gonna do, say, "the school isn't doing this, but they've got 70 per cent five A to Cs"? You know, where are they gonna, where are they gonna draw the line? You know, for me it's all about the students in this community, the school community and the wider community, being able to change their lives and being able to change their families' and their communities' lives. And you don't do that always by playing by the rules.'

> 'Attendance targets – very difficult. They're very difficult to get, attendance targets. But to be honest, you know, if you don't get them, what's going to happen? Again, you know, who's going to come and arrest us?'

However further discussion revealed that Mr Weller's 'resistance' amounted to getting some extra training days for staff in exceptional circumstances and around which he had undertaken consultation with parents. Thus despite his exceptionally 'brave' talk, Mr Weller did not have a very fundamental challenge to policy in mind, and was in any case carefully 'covering' himself:

> 'I've stolen days this year for training. You know, you're not supposed – you're supposed to teach a certain amount of days, this year I've stolen days. There was an – we were supposed to do an extra day this year, but I've given it because we got an achievement award last year I've given – it didn't quite fit into the year plan. I would have had to open school for a Monday somewhere. So, I said "it's ridiculous". So, what I've written to governors and staff about, and parents, I said that I'm actually – because we got a school achievement award, I'm giving everybody an extra day's holiday. So, you know, they might say, "you're not teaching enough, you're

not open enough days of the year". But at the beginning of the year I steal a couple of days for extra training. And we have Year 7s come in for a couple of hours, one day Year 10s come in for a couple of hours, but actually the rest of the staff are training. So, we do – we actually have four days before school starts at the beginning of the year, which helps us to settle everything down, get schemes of work ready, induct new staff. Make sure we're not doing everything at the last minute – it isn't a rush, people are less stressed when they start teaching, and I think that's very important so that the children get a good start. So, there's lots of things we do which are bending the rules or breaking the rules – blatantly in some situations. But I think I can justify it, I'm not [...] And I do pay lip-service to the rules. You know, I will, I will write letters to parents saying that, you know, "is it okay if we do this?" You know, I don't think Ofsted will count them up. But if they do, we just need to cover ourselves. We cover ourselves, I think, is what we do.'

Mr Weller's account illustrates that when heads talk about filtering policy it may not amount to much. More generally the Wyeham study suggested that heads are very much caught within the discourses of OSI. Again Mr Weller provides a good example when his discussion of creativity gives way to an emphasis on target setting:

'We ask for creative teaching, so they have to have a bit of inventiveness, a bit of creativity in what they are doing. But they also have to be able to manage the classroom, they have to say this is correct, this is incorrect, they have to be aware of somebody, you know, Perry, in the corner who might not be working. And they have to pick that up and deal with it.'

'I want us to be focusing on literacy, I want us to be focusing on achievement and bringing students from level four to level five. I want to know, if a child is coming from level four they must be going to level five. If they are not going to level five why isn't it? What do they need to get there? The parents need to know that, the kids need to know that, and we've got a new target setting system to try and make that happen. So I really believe that the school is set to take off. I thought it might happen this year, probably not, in terms of the results. But I think it will happen in the very near future.'

Teachers responses to OSI

Whether teachers respond to OSI any more critically than heads is unclear. On the one hand, teachers have been reformed many times over, initial teacher education under New Labour hardly sets up a critical perspective (Furlong *et al.* 2000) and teachers are also under considerable pressure to go along with OSI because of the demands of Ofsted inspections (both their own rating and that of the school collectively) and of performance management which is tied to student achievement targets. On the other hand they are less directly worked upon by New Labour (although they are targeted by new NCSL programmes such as Leading from the Middle) and being closer to the chalkface, are perhaps more likely to recognize how OSI policy is failing to meet the needs of many students.

It may be older teachers, those who trained and taught before the development of OSI, who are most critical. While heads sometimes talk with frustration about the 'dinosaurs' among their teaching staff, it is likely that some of the teachers so-characterized are welfarist teachers who remain unconvinced by OSI. Related to this point, earlier accounts of teachers contesting reform may be too optimistic for today. The writers on teachers contesting reform noted in Chapter 1 (Osborne and Broadfoot 1992; Woods 1995) were relatively upbeat about the ability of England's teachers to 'speak back' to reform. However as the decade progressed and managerialist trends became more dominant they often became less confident that teachers would win through. For instance Hargreaves (1998) reviewed *Restructuring Schools, Reconstructing Teachers* (Woods *et al.* 1997) and observed that the picture painted by Woods and colleagues was 'particularly sobering' when much of Woods' work in the past had attempted to locate and even celebrate teachers who were resisting top-down reform:

> The vast majority of the primary teachers the research team studied have been patently ground down, worn out, demoralized, profes-sionally diminished, drained of their passion and robbed of their optimism and hope. More depressing still, the few exceptions who do appear able to prosper and remain positive despite, or even because of, the reforms, seem less like shrewd resisters than career

opportunists (all of them have positions of responsibility ...) or apologists for the new system. (Hargreaves, 1998: 420–21)

Other recent accounts also provide a bleaker assessment of the potential for teacher contestation than the research from a decade or more ago. Drawing on survey research about schools' and teachers' preferences for teacher professional development, Bottery and Wright (2000) argue that that not only do teachers apparently have little understanding or interest in wider 'ecological' areas, but schools do little in terms of their staff's continuing professional development in relation to them. Bottery (2000) concludes that the response of teachers to educational reform in England has been

> very cautionary ... they exhibited a potentially dangerous mixture of overwork and indifference towards an understanding of why these changes had come about, and what they as professionals should do in reaction to them. (Bottery 2000: 223)

According to Bottery (2000) the reasons for this are that the vast majority of teachers see their role as centrally concerned with either 'the kids' or 'the subject' and are uncomfortable about taking a political stance, particularly in the light of the damaging teacher strikes of the 1980s. Drawing on Hargreaves and Goodson (1996), Bottery and Wright (2000: 98–9) argue that a key problem is the various models of professionalism on which teachers draw that together form a restricted view of professionalism. For instance 'flexible professionalism' encourages teachers to connect to local communities and 'practical professionalism' emphasizes knowledge of teaching as a craft but these models may prevent teachers from 'fully appreciating the wider forces impacting upon them' and 'prevent reflection by the teaching profession on ... wider ecological issues'.

Gale and Densmore (2003: 87) also note how teacher professionalism may prevent teachers from being searching about issues of social justice in school reform:

> The professional is traditionally exhorted to remain detached from, in contrast to committed to, social ideas and values, on the assumption that this detachment permits objectivity. Professional ideology and the training they receive in teacher education programmes can hold

educators back from identifying with ... low-income students of colour for whom (standard) English is a second language. Further some educators tend to be uncomfortable with the language of power. ... Certainly the notion that 'all students can succeed' is inspiring, but it is not helpful when it ignores the importance of non-school related influences on school success.

Gale and Densmore (p. 91) go on to note how teachers are also prevented from taking a wider view of their profession-alism because of the managerial school environment discussed in Chapter 2. First, teachers are becoming too isolated to be exposed to other perspectives:

Being a professional teacher in [a context of competitive individu-alism] amounts to the effective and efficient performance of one's duties but there is little room for considering the worth of these, especially in collaboration with others.

Second, managerialism leads to the closing down of debate:

The sticks and carrots of corporate managerialism ... contribute to an arrogant purchase on knowledge and action that isolates and contains dissension. Work intensification, a limited scope for decision making, and the imperative to be a market leader – the 'manufactured' compression of time – also contribute to a lack of debate. There is less time for interaction and for questioning the value of current practices, producing a 'fast' professionalism.

Third, there is a reduction of meaningful work 'where teachers' and teacher-educators' expertise is frequently dismissed and oppor-tunities to contribute to working through social and institutional problems are appropriated by management'.

Despite all the problems they highlight, Gale and Densmore do hold out the possibility of a more progressive teaching force, yet like the 'mediating headteachers' work noted above, their account seems to be more aspirational than anything else.

Issues of methodology and scope

The arguments in favour of heads 'mediating' reform do not hold up well against the counter-arguments of Wright, Hatcher and Bottery that heads and teachers mostly comply with reform. Indeed without better evidence of policy actually being mediated, mediation seems mostly an article of faith in the discussions of Day, Earley, Gold and colleagues. Yet the arguments of Wright, Hatcher and Bottery against heads and teachers contesting OSI also have the important limitation of not engaging *closely* with the perspectives and activities of practitioners. Getting up close is likely to be important because Menter and colleagues (1997) argue that managerial discourses 'manufacture consent' to reform and point to a gap between 'the model of the responsible, accountable professional on public display and the private experience of bitterness, anxiety and overload' (p. 115). If this is the case, it is possible that heads and teachers are privately much more willing to contest OSI than they publicly seem to be.

The contribution of the next chapter to this debate is to illustrate that there are important ways OSI could be quietly contested in schools, with some anecdotal evidence that this is happening. However the issue really requires more research and of a particular kind, namely ethnographic methods which allow the researcher to get beyond 'what is said' to 'what is done' by immersion in school life over an extended period of time so as to become a trusted confidant for heads or teachers. Unfortunately the time commitment involved in such research makes it hard for academics to obtain funding for or do well, although covert practices in response to OSI policies could be the subject of very useful doctoral research.

A further issue is the scope of the above debates as they do not consider the role of national teacher and headteacher unions or professional associations. The NCSL is relevant here because if it is mainly relaying OSI policy we could ask why headteacher organizations are supportive of it. We need to look at how critical the perspectives of such national organizations are and to what extent they contest OSI and again this is considered in Chapter 5.

5   Best keep down here

They went in single file – first Mr Beaver, then Lucy, then Peter, then Susan, and Mrs Beaver last of all. Mr Beaver led them across the dam and on to the right bank of the river and then along a very rough sort of path among the trees right down by the river-bank. The sides of the valley, shining in the moonlight, towered up far above them on either side. 'Best keep down here as much as possible,' he said. 'She'll have to keep to the top, for you couldn't bring a sledge down here.' (from *The Lion, the Witch and the Wardrobe* by C.S. Lewis)

Like the second half of the previous chapter, this chapter is concerned with practitioner contestation of OSI but it explores a much wider range of activity. I begin with a general discussion of the strengths and limitations of different kinds of contestation along a spectrum from national and regional activities to those carried out more locally by individual schools and the staff within them. Approaches to contesting reform at these different levels are then considered in more detail. As noted in the last chapter, research is badly needed in the area of covert practices which allow individuals and groups within schools to contest OSI but there are some examples which illustrate that along with more public activity there are many ways OSI could be, and probably is being, surreptitiously undermined.

The pros and cons of contesting OSI at different levels

As noted in Chapter 1, contestation as used in this book is intended to be a widely inclusive term. It represents a spectrum of activities at different levels, from those which are national or regional and therefore typically more public, to those which are more local and often likely to remain hidden. Approaches to contesting reform at all of these levels have strengths and limitations and the argument here is not for one form of contestation over others but for using multiple approaches and using the most effective approach for any particular problem.

National or regional forms of contestation of OSI have the obvious advantage of strength in numbers. They can have more impact on policy and practice than the actions of individual schools and reduce the risk of members being picked off as an 'isolated case'. By their nature, such forms of contestation also tend to be in the public eye, which again has the advantage of delivering a clear message to central or local government that a policy or initiative is problematic. They can also spur wider political action by providing an example for other practitioners. Nevertheless being large scale and public has its drawbacks. National action involves different constituencies amongst whom it may be difficult to achieve agreement over more far-reaching contestation, particularly when the political consequences for individuals and the organization of engaging openly in such activities may be dire. All of this means that where critique is to be followed by practice, national activities are typically used where there is still room to manoeuvre openly because reforms are not yet embedded in legislation or are not compulsory.

Public contestation at the level of the individual school or its staff shares the same limitation of being too exposed to contest compulsory policy through practice. Its other key limitation is that without strength of numbers, a school and or the individuals within it can be more vulnerable. However this form of contestation can highlight problems in OSI which are well raised by the case of a single school or individual and may be useful either where there is no wider campaign about an issue or to supplement that campaign.

The main advantage of local and covert contestation of OSI is that it can allow practitioners to undertake practices which would be difficult to carry out publicly because they actively work against the requirements of OSI. But the same lack of transparency makes it important to consider the motives which lie behind local covert activities. The problem is that practices which have the effect of contesting reform may not always stem from educational or social justice concerns but from more personally opportunistic motives. Conversely, practices which seem intended to benefit the individual can stem from wider ethical concerns, for instance action to protect one's own reputation may also be intended to protect a school from special measures or closure. For practitioners it is crucial to reflect on whether covert practices which work against OSI are really justifiable for educational or social justice reasons or whether other motives come into play. From a research perspective, while it is possible to point to many examples of *possible* covert contestation, it is rarely clear *why* people acted in the ways they did. To make a more confident claim for contestation of OSI, research needs to contextualize particular actions within a wider account of the perspectives and practices of the school or people concerned.

Contesting OSI – a spectrum of activities

The following discussion considers contestation of OSI from the national to the local level and from public to covert actions. It is not intended to be exhaustive, but includes many of the ways OSI is likely to be being contested at present.

Union and professional association activity

Teacher and headteacher unions and professional associations vary considerably in the extent to which they take up issues that go wider than pay and working conditions and hence generate and legitimize contestation of OSI among their members. However, along the lines discussed above, they are all more likely to emphasize issues of developing concern (such as the introduction of performance-related pay or workforce remodelling) rather than taking action over long-standing or established elements of OSI (such as SATs testing or Ofsted inspections). In the latter case, membership support for action may be limited, both because the established reforms have become acceptable to many members and because openly refusing to comply could have serious consequences. There has also been an important history in England of governments exerting powerful controls over the teaching profession, leaving their unions and associations in a much weakened position. For instance, under the Conservatives there was a long pay dispute in the 1980s followed by the Teachers Pay and Conditions Act (1987) which effectively deprived teachers of their right to negotiate salaries and conditions of service. Today most of these organizations try to maintain 'constructive dialogue' with government wherever possible so they pick their battles carefully.

Here I shall compare and contrast the stance and activities of the NUT, NASUWT, SHA and NAHT, four of the main education unions/professional associations.[1] The National Union of Teachers (NUT, www.teachers.org.uk) has both teacher and headteacher members. It is the oldest and largest of the unions/professional associations and also the most critical of OSI. Its website includes information about the 'commercialization' and 'privatization' of education, and its press releases are often harder hitting and more critical in tone than the other teacher and headteacher organizations/associations discussed here, for instance:

> NUT slams education choice
>
> The head of the NUT has criticized government proposals aimed at increasing school choice for parents. Speaking hours before education secretary Charles Clarke's five-year schools policy was put to the Commons today, Steve Sinnott said the plans would lead to selection within state schools. 'We believe that when you have a choice of the sort that is being banded about at the moment, it ends up with schools being able to select the youngsters rather than the parents selecting the school for the youngsters,' he told the Today programme. 'We don't want schools to be able to weed out those youngsters who are from the less advantaged backgrounds and who might depress a school's tests or examination results.' Mr Sinnott has previously expressed concern over the planned expansion of semi-independent city academies, a flagship government policy. Charles Clarke today pledged to increase schools' independence and said he would like to see all secondary schools become specialist in the same time period. (NUT Press release 08/07/2004)

The NUT responded to the Government's Five Year Strategy for Children and Learners by launching its own five-year strategy for education, entitled *Bringing Down the Barriers* (NUT 2004).

This called for a review of the National Curriculum to remove the distinction between core and foundation subjects, an end to selection, targets, league tables and Key Stage tests; and replacing Ofsted with a restructured HMI.

In 2003 the NUT was noteworthy for refusing to be part of the National Agreement on workload signed by many other teacher organizations, including all the others discussed here. Its main concern was the planned use of teaching assistants without teaching qualifications to address teacher workload by taking some classes. It took out advertisements in the *TES* which criticized the NASUWT and other unions for signing up to the National Agreement. In response, in an article called 'Has the NUT gone nuts?' posted on the NASUWT website, the NASUWT claimed that the NUT has become 'the mouthpiece of ultra-left factions which dominate its National Executive ... totally unrepresentative of teacher opinion in general'. It then painted a disastrous picture of the record of the NUT in recent years, including the following:

- this is the union that opposed the introduction of the Threshold arrangements back in 1998, went to Court in order to prevent their payment to the thousands and thousands of deserving teachers, lost the Court case but succeeded in delaying the payment of the Threshold for many months;
- this is the union that claimed the overwhelming majority of its members would vote to support a boycott of Key Stages 1 and 2, but then ignominiously lost the vote; and
- this is the union that engages relentlessly in the rhetoric of militancy but consistently fails to make good its promises about militant action.

Leaving aside the tone of all this, what it does point to are some of the difficulties the NUT has faced in taking a strong stance against OSI, including lack of support from its own members and wider disregard for its stance as too left-wing.

For its own part the National Association of Schoolmasters Union of Women Teachers (NASUWT, www.teachersunion.org.uk), with over 220,000 teacher and headteacher members, argues it is not one of the 'Government's unions' as the NUT has positioned it but rather 'engaged in serious negotiations, as any self-respecting union would seek to do'. Nevertheless, what it considers it has achieved over the last few years is telling. For instance, a web article called 'NASUWT – Making a Difference', argues that the NASUWT has 'secured the reduction of the main scale from 9 to 6 points to improve salaries for younger teachers; seized the opportunity presented by the introduction of threshold to secure additional money for teachers and engaged with Government to secure considerable improvements on the original proposals and developed a strategy, which included appropriate industrial action in individual schools, to ensure that the vast majority of eligible teachers moved to UPS2'. It argues that as a result of these strategies, it achieved 'an additional £10,625 for teachers outside London who applied for threshold in September 2000 and moved to UPS2 in September 2002 and for inner-London teachers progressing on the same timescale, an additional £11,666'. It also suggests it has achieved 'recognition of the crucially important role of classroom teachers in raising standards and the need for them to be free to focus on teaching; the removal of administrative and clerical tasks from teachers; and the provision of leadership and management time within school sessions for all teachers who have these responsibilities, paid or unpaid'.

These are considerable achievements but they provide a strong sense of the NASUWT trying to improve pay and conditions for teachers who work within OSI, rather than challenging the tenets of OSI itself as the NUT has often been concerned to do. Perhaps the NASUWT is only able to show more success for its efforts because it takes a more supportive stance towards OSI in the first place. Compared to the NUT's response to the DfES's Five Year Strategy, the NASUWT's response suggests there is some truth in this conclusion but also that NASUWT policy is not only about tinkering at the margins. It aims to remove league tables, avoid a two-tier system of provision around specialist schooling and selection, and raises numerous concerns about Academies, and the impact of PFI (NASUWT 2004). However rather than putting up an alternative agenda informed by a strong concern for social justice like the NUT's, the NASUWT's approach is to work with government to try to have some influence over policy:

> The provisions embodied in the Strategy are designed to ensure that all children are able to benefit from the highest quality education and realize their full potential. This is an ambition shared by NASUWT. There is a clear recognition in the Strategy that teachers, heads and other members of the school workforce are of crucial importance in achieving this goal and that they require training, support and resources to enable them to continue to work effectively and to the highest standards. This is extremely welcome. There are, however, some very difficult issues raised in the Strategy which require detailed discussion and consideration. The continuation of the constructive dialogue in which the Government has engaged over the last three years with school workforce unions will be essential to the achievement of a mutually satisfactory resolution of these issues. (NASUWT 2004: 12)

As noted above, the two headteacher organizations considered here, SHA and the NAHT, were both also parties to the workforce agreement and in most respects share a similar approach to working with government as the NASUWT. With some 10,000 members, the Secondary Heads Association (SHA, www.sha.org. uk) has criticised school league tables every year and suggested changes to examinations and assessment, especially promoting the notion of 'intelligent accountability' as an alternative to the OSI approach (SHA 2003; SHA 2004). Its press releases have criticized the promotion of diversity between schools, Ofsted's identification of 'failing schools', enterprise education and business involvement in schools. In 2002 it balloted its members with a view to boycotting PRP (the first national ballot in its history). Nevertheless, on balance SHA seems to agree with, or wants to be seen to agree with, the thrust of OSI. For every press release criticizing aspects of OSI policy there are many more praising elements of it. Here is its response to the Five Year Strategy:

Secondary Heads give strong welcome to greater autonomy for heads and school funding reforms

On Tuesday 6 July, the Secondary Heads Association issued a press release outlining the policies which it hoped to see in the government's five-year strategy document, published today. SHA is pleased to see the inclusion of the following policies, many of which it has sought for many years: greater autonomy for secondary heads; ring-fenced funding for LEAs to ensure that government education money is devolved to schools; greater stability and predictability in funding, with a renewed commitment to introduce three-year budgets based on the academic year; a single school improvement grant to replace the present multiple funding streams to schools; an acceleration of the specialist schools programme; no new categories of schools; no increase in selection and the continuation of existing admission arrangements; strong support for schools on dealing with bad behaviour; schools working collaboratively on exclusions and behaviour policies; strong commitment to the success of the new relationship with schools, leading to a rationalization and reduction in the multiple accountabilities currently facing head teachers, and schools to set targets at key stages 3 and 4 (bottom-up), instead of targets being imposed by the government and LEAs in a top-down model.

SHA General Secretary, Dr John Dunford, commented: 'Secondary heads will be pleased that the government has given them a vote of confidence with more autonomy for individual schools and a clearer funding mechanism to enable them to plan their budgets better. Ring-fenced funding and three-year budgets should bring an end to the problems of the present system in which the government and local authorities blame each other when anything goes wrong and schools are left to sort out the difficulties. These are important steps towards the fairer funding system that SHA has long sought. Schools play a vital part in their wider local communities and the strategy contains some important measures in which schools will be expected to work together. This collaboration is an important component in a successful local education system. It is essential that academies work with other local schools for the benefit of all young people in the area. The success of the academies programme must be judged not only on their own results, but by their effect on the performance of all the local schools. The government must ensure that the academies' independence does not work against the interests of other local schools. It remains our view that the cost of building academies should be cut. If 200 academies are built at the present average cost of £25 million each, this £5 billion will use too much of available capital funds.' (SHA Press release 08/07/2004)

Finally the National Association of Headteachers (NAHT, www. naht.org.uk) with over 30,000 members has also campaigned against 'high stakes' SATs testing and league tables and expressed concern about Ofsted inspections. With SHA it also balloted its members with a view to boycotting PRP (its only national ballot in the last 20 years). Nevertheless the NAHT's criticisms of OSI are again made within a generally supportive discourse, for instance:

Government's Five-Year Education Action Plan Makes A Great Deal Of Sense Says NAHT

David Hart, General Secretary NAHT comments on the Government's five-year education plan, published today, as follows: 'The Government's five-year education plan makes a great deal of sense. We back greater independence for schools. Guaranteed three-year funding is precisely what heads need if they are going to deliver higher standards. More autonomy, less red tape and a crack-down on both bad pupil and bad parent behaviour is exactly what heads need. Expanding popular schools, closing unsuccessful schools and creating more academies may well appeal electorally. But an unlicensed education market could all too easily damage the education of pupils in those schools that descend into an irretrievable spiral of decline. We welcome the Government's plan for the under-fives. It is an exciting vision of how primary schools can deliver high-quality education and childcare, not just in the most deprived areas, but across the country as a whole. Schools that are open from early morning to evening would meet the heavy demand for pre-school and childcare. But heads will require substantial capital and revenue funding if this very significant challenge is to be met.' (NAHT Press release 8 July 2004)

Overall, with all of these unions/professional associations trying to combat at least the worst elements of OSI, it is clear that practitioner involvement in such organizations is a useful way of contesting at least some elements of OSI. There are differences in the level of critique developed by the different organizations with the NASUWT, SHA and the NAHT all more willing to work with OSI than the NUT.

An important goal for those who want to contest OSI through the former could be to press for a stronger critique. The means of achieving this would vary according to the politics of the specific organization concerned but may be very much a case of timing and recognizing the issues on which wider contestation amongst colleagues could be built. For instance in March 2005 Ruth Kelly was reported as getting the coldest reception from heads at a SHA conference of any education secretary in the last quarter century (Taylor 2005). Heads were angry and frustrated that her election pledge that schools would teach students in small groups was setting up expectations among parents which were completely unrealistic within existing resources. Handled well, such events can be used to highlight other areas where the government is not listening to educational and social justice concerns. The need to develop a more critical stance on policy is less an issue for NUT members. Especially when other unions and professional associations are willing to mostly go with government policy, it is clearly a tightrope act for the NUT to take a strong stance against OSI but not do too much damage in terms of political positioning and membership support.

National pressure and interest groups

Along with unions and professional associations, there are a number of other national groups, foundations and associations which provide practitioners with avenues for contesting OSI. One of the most important in terms of the themes of this book is the Campaign for State Education (CASE, www.casenet.org.uk) which campaigns in support of state comprehensive education and hence against selection and privatization. There are also research associations like BERA (the British Educational Research Association, www.bera.ac.uk) and groups with more specific concerns like the Institute of Race Relations (IRR, www.irr.org.uk) which is especially concerned with institutionalized racism and responding to the needs of Black people, and the Communities Empowerment

Network (CEN, www.compowernet.org) which has a particular focus on school exclusions.

Another example of a way forward for practitioners is provided by the National Primary Headteachers Association (NphA, www. primaryheads.org.uk) which despite its name does not seek to take on the roles and responsibilities of the established unions and associations discussed earlier. It is a lobby group made up of serving primary headteachers in England which was formed in 1995 after primary heads gave evidence at the House of Commons on funding disparities between primary and secondary schools. Although not as critical as the other organizations in this section, it is concerned with moving from 'SATuration to Sensible Assessment' and as part of the National Primary Education Alliance (NPEA) is promoting alternatives to SATs. Its web editorial invites members to take control of school reform:

> This issue of NPhA News attempts to look at the marginalization of the Foundation subjects and how they can play an effective part in a broad and balanced curriculum. It also seeks to present you with a golden opportunity to 'capture' your own dream ticket for your school. Ofsted are in the process of piloting the 'new' future form of inspection based on 'Every Child Matters'. Workload Reforms loom on the horizon. The Primary Strategy 'Teaching and Learning' document is also launched this term. This is your opportunity to grasp the nettle and create that vision which is particular for your school. Miss this chance and the way ahead will remain unclear and shrouded in doubt and obstacles. Why not view Workload Reform as a way of thinking 'outside the box'? Make it work for you. Be assertive and do not let the tail wag the dog ... (from NPhA website editorial).

All of these (and other) groups make a contribution, but in terms of 'joined-up thinking', a UK version of the US 'Rethinking Schools' organization (www.rethinkingschools.org) would be particularly helpful. Rethinking Schools was initially a local organization set up by a group of Milwaukee teachers in 1986 to address problems such as standardized testing and a textbook-dominated curriculum. Today it has subscribers in all 50 US states and many other countries and publishes numerous texts and on-line resources including its flagship journal *Rethinking Schools*. The following is taken from the Rethinking Schools website:

> While the scope and influence of Rethinking Schools has changed, its basic orientation has not. Most importantly, it remains firmly committed to equity and to the vision that public education is central to the creation of a humane, caring, multiracial democracy. While writing for a broad audience, Rethinking Schools emphasizes problems facing urban schools, particularly issues of race.
>
> Throughout its history, Rethinking Schools has tried to balance classroom practice and educational theory. It is an activist publication, with articles written by and for teachers, parents, and students. Yet it also addresses key policy issues, such as vouchers and marketplace-oriented reforms, funding equity, and school-to-work.
>
> Rethinking Schools attempts to be both visionary and practical: visionary because we need to be inspired by each other's vision of schooling; practical because for too long, teachers and parents have been preached at by theoreticians, far-removed from classrooms, who are long on jargon and short on specific examples.
>
> At a time when racial and class inequalities are growing in our country, we believe that any vision of schooling must be grounded in 'the common school'. Schools are about more than producing efficient workers or future winners of the Nobel Prize for science. They are the place in this society where children from a variety of backgrounds come together and, at least in theory, learn to talk, play, and work together.
>
> Schools are integral not only to preparing all children to be full participants in society, but also to be full participants in this country's ever-tenuous experiment in democracy. That this vision has yet to be fully realized does not mean it should be abandoned.
>
> There are many reasons to be discouraged about the future: School districts nationwide continue to slash budgets; violence in our schools and cities shows no signs of abating; attempts to privatize the schools have not slowed; and the country's productive resources are still used to make zippier shoes, rather than used in less profitable arenas like education and affordable housing.
>
> There is a Zulu expression: 'If the future doesn't come toward you, you have to go fetch it.' We believe teachers, parents, and students are essential to building a movement to go fetch a better

future: in our classrooms, in our schools, and in the larger society. There are lots of us out there. Let's make our voices heard.

In December 2004 a diverse group of educators met in London around the theme 'Another school is possible' and in March 2005 another broad-based education coalition put together a day seminar on 'Rethinking education in the era of globalisation'. This looks set to spawn an organization like 'Rethinking Schools' but tailored to respond to the particular constraints and possibilities of England's OSI environment (see www.rethinked.org.uk).

Finally, an important and necessary strength of all of the above organizations is their formal independence of government. This point needs to be made because there are increasing opportunities for practitioners to join government-sponsored interest groups. One of these is the Leadership Network launched by the NCSL in 2002 with the intent of 'establishing a direct connection between school leaders and government in policy development ... it is hoped that the network will eventually advise government on education policy' (NCSL website – Leadership Network page). Perhaps there is some opportunity to influence policy here but at present the Network seems to be being heavily shaped by policy-makers and by key figures in the (conventional) school effectiveness and school improvement movement:

> current themes of enquiry for the Network are system leadership, personalized learning, professional learning and within school variation. ... The within school variation work began in 2003 when a group of over 30 schools drawn from the network worked with Professor David Reynolds of Exeter University and staff from NCSL, DfES and the Innovation Unit. ... Professor David Hopkins introduced the notion of personalized learning at the Network's first national conference. Network members are represented on DfES working groups and are providing operational images to support policy development in leading the person-centred school. ... This year's [annual conference for the Leadership Network] was held on 12 October at the Birmingham NEC on the theme of 'Leading Personalization in Schools'. Among the speakers were David Miliband, Charles Leadbeater and Dean Fink. (From NCSL website, Leadership Network page)

Collaboration among groups of schools

Collective public contestation can also occur at a relatively small-scale level. For example Grace (2002) provides some empirical findings about organized collaboration between school leaders in Catholic schools as a way of contesting market 'realities' and working towards the common good. He points in particular to the Birmingham Catholic Secondary Partnership which involves formal collaboration amongst ten schools over enrolments, school improvement and a host of other matters. Grace argues that such developments represent a 'developed countercultural force' to the market in education. Indeed he found '[e]xplicit condemnation of the potentially corrupting effects of market values and market forces in Catholic education' characterized the stance of at least half of the 60 heads he interviewed in London, Liverpool and Birmingham between 1997–9 (p. 197). These heads were 'searching for forms of association and collaboration which would meet reasonable demands for efficiency and accountability ... while not involving the "win or die" imperatives of unregulated market competition in schooling' (p. 204). Such collaboration does not have to be just a feature of the Catholic school system and actually many of the Catholic heads in Grace's study were more willing to go along with market competition.

School collaboration is another area where government is increasingly involved, for instance through the Primary Strategy Learning Networks mentioned in Chapter 3. Plans for these networks need to be approved by the DfES but may offer some opportunity to move away from the OSI agenda towards more searching concerns.

Refusing (non-compulsory) reforms

Moving now to the level of individual schools, these and the staff within them can openly refuse to take up OSI policies which are not compulsory. For instance over the period 1997–2002 a number of secondary schools chose not to apply for Specialist status on the grounds that such a system would intensify inequalities between schools. Phipps (2004) reports the case of Tony Neal, headteacher of De Aston School, who argued publicly in 2001 that 'we are treating one set of schools as high status, high funded and another as low status, low funded. ... It clearly isn't fair to be regarding half the pupils in the country as second-class citizens.' In 2002 the government lifted the funding cap to allow all schools to become specialist schools, thus removing Neal's main objection and his school and others have now gone into the scheme, although a small number of schools are still keeping their distance because of various concerns (Phipps 2004).

A related issue is whether or not specialist schools should select the 10 per cent of students they are allowed to. Our EU research in Wyeham found one secondary school where it was immediately ruled out by the governing body:

Governor: (Our school) doesn't select at all.
Interviewer: No. Even though it's got specialist status?
Governor: Even though.
Interviewer: So, it would be entitled to.
Governor: It was a ten second conversation at governors' ...
Interviewer: Was it?
Governor: Yeah, it was, 'we're not gonna band are we?' 'No'.
Move on.

Such decisions are rarely highlighted by schools but nor are they hidden. It is a case of schools acting within the discretion they have both legally and performatively. It may be argued that the main reason schools have discretion and are able to mediate policy in this instance is because the outcome of the decision is of little interest to the DfES or Ofsted or in most cases, the community served by the school. Put another way, many specialist schools are unlikely to really regret or be disadvantaged by the decision not to select 10 per cent while for those not yet specialist (particularly rural schools) there seems to be little to gain in specialist status apart from the extra funding it brings (Phipps 2004).

Critique and textual dissent

Criticism of OSI need not be restricted to academics, nor to the unions and professional organizations already discussed. As I noted in my earlier book with Rob Willmott (Thrupp and Willmott 2003), it is helpful when heads are open about unpalatable decisions they have to make around school budgets, staffing, marketing and the like so as to problematize OSI rather than obscure it by absorbing these problems themselves. It also helps if they are well-informed (what does research show us?), savvy enough to assess the political risk of particular activities (what can we get away with?) and able to use a mix of convincing argument, humour and sarcasm to get their message across (why is this kind of reform not to be taken seriously but also very seriously?) For instance the head who comes into the staffroom and begins the discussion of some 'important' activity such as SATs testing with the quip 'more pig weighing today unfortunately folks' (as in the Confucian saying 'No matter how often you weigh a pig it doesn't make it any fatter') is delivering the message to staff that 'we are doing this because we have to but I want you to keep a wider perspective'. Similarly, heads and teachers who are able to talk with confidence to parents about the limitations of market, managerial, performative and prescriptive reforms in education and able to convincingly illustrate how their school is trying to take a more clearly educational stance, should be able to gather considerable support even in aspirant, middle-class communities.

Forms of critical writing about OSI – textual dissent – including opinion pieces, letters, articles and submissions can also be written by individuals or small groups of staff. All such dissenting accounts help to keep the issues in front of other practitioners and their organizations, the media, public and policy-makers, building a climate of concern which may lead to shifts in policy or more fundamental change. The *Times Educational Supplement* is widely read and influential in the education sector, while *Improving Schools* is a progressive school improvement journal which invites contributions from practitioners.

Legal challenges

Some individuals and schools have taken education agencies to court as a means of protesting against OSI policies. In particular, Ofsted inspections have been the subject of an increasing number of legal challenges (Hill 2004). The best-known case of successful legal action against Ofsted was in 2000 at Summerhill, the famous progressive school founded by A.S. Neill, where the school appealed against a notice of complaint by then Education and Employment Secretary David Blunkett, issued after an Ofsted report had found serious weaknesses. Summerhill was reprieved and costs paid by the DfES after its legal counsel told an independent schools tribunal that a report by an independent expert team had 'left no doubt whatsoever that the work of Ofsted was incompetent, biased and distorted' (Mansell 2000b; Dean 2000).

Public resignations and stepping back from the job

There have been cases of practitioners publicly 'falling on their sword' by resigning in protest at some element of OSI. Ofsted inspections have triggered a number of resignations from seemingly competent heads, for instance this story from the *TES* (Burnham 2002):

Community shocked as head resigns over report

A school community has been left distraught by the resignation of its head following an inspectors' report that criticized his leadership.

The chairman of the governors said governors, staff, parents and pupils wept openly when they learned of the departure of Jim Abraham, who has been in charge of the award-winning school for 23 years. He decided to take early retirement at the age of 56 after he read a draft report of the inspection that described his leadership as 'not satisfactory'.

Parents of children at Arthur Dye, in Cheltenham, Gloucestershire, this week have been queuing up to beg him to reconsider his decision to quit.

Kate Bingham, who sent her three children to the school, said: 'He's an old-fashioned teacher who teaches his pupils to care about each other. He has done a wonderful job. You cannot afford to lose people like him.'

Kevin Samuelson, a father of four, said: 'I have nothing but praise for the man. He is such a good headteacher. It is such a waste of a man with so much experience.'

Inspectors from the Office for Standards in Education visited the school last month. Their final report is expected in September.

In an emotional letter to parents, Mr Abraham said: 'The inspectors spoke in glowing terms about a lot of the things that are happening here. But they decided they didn't like my leadership.

'It seems they either want a strong head, who is leading teachers as if they have rings through their noses, or one who is whipping them from behind. Well I cannot work like that. I regard myself as part of a band of professionals who work together and I can't sign up to anything else.'

Mr Abraham told the TES that the inspectors' comments were the final straw after he had battled against changing education strategies.

'When I started in teaching in the late Sixties, teaching was a wonderful, exciting job,' he said. 'But not any more. Teachers are no longer able to exercise the freedom of their own professional judgement.

'The curriculum has become ridiculously overloaded. We shouldn't be filling little children with facts and making them feel their every move is being judged by an exam. Results have come to mean so much to the status of a school that the majority have sacrificed a balanced curriculum.'

Bill Riley, chairman of governors, described Mr Abraham's decision as 'tragic' and criticized the inspectors who visited the school. He said: 'He is determined to go. He has been pushed too far by nincompoops.'

In the school's last Ofsted report in 1997, Mr Abraham was praised for his 'strong pastoral leadership'. And in both 2001 and 2002, Arthur Dye won School Achievement Awards for standards gained by pupils and staff.

Mr Abraham decided to quit after reading the draft report, which he was sent to check for factual accuracy.

An Ofsted spokeswoman said: 'We cannot comment on this case until the school receives the final inspection report.'

The 'Fresh Start' initiative has also led to public resignations by heads, both when schools are given notice they will be 'Fresh Started' (e.g. Mansell and Hackett 2000) and resignations by Fresh Start heads themselves (e.g. Mansell 2000c). The latter case was the high-profile resignations of three Fresh Start 'superheads' within five days in March 2000 after Blunkett announced tough 'floor targets' for failing schools. These targets were outlined in a speech to the Social Market Foundation in which Blunkett argued that 'by 2004 there should be no secondary school anywhere with less than 20 per cent of its pupils achieving 5A*-Cs.' (Blunkett 2000b).

Some of the above heads had other positions lined up before resigning but some did not. In the latter case, the personal cost of publicly 'walking the plank' can be huge and has to be counted as another cost of OSI as well as a form of contesting it.

It is also likely that OSI policies have led vast numbers of heads and teachers to step back from their job in various ways including quietly resigning, taking early retirement, going part time, refusing promotion or taking up a less senior position. Although the 20,000 or so teachers who resign from English schools each year mostly complain about excessive workload ('Teachers to quit in droves' 2000; Slater 2003d), it is OSI which creates intensification. For instance Mansell (2001c) highlights the case of Moorlands Primary in Reading where nearly 30 per cent of staff, (five of 16 teachers) left at the end of the 2001 year. In a letter to the *TES* the remaining teachers listed nine reasons why their colleagues were leaving. They included constant paperwork and frustration at constant government initiatives with 'insufficient time, training and resources to accomplish what is expected' and being overloaded with 'inappropriate' curricula.

Teachers are also often retiring as early as possible. Thornton (2002b) reported that more than a quarter of the teachers who retired in 2002 did so early with nearly half of those quitting early doing so at the earliest opportunity, aged 55 or 56. Early retirement is popular in spite of the (Conservative) government having taken steps in 1997 to halt the spiralling cost of early retirement to central government by making schools, colleges and local authorities partly responsible for pension costs. Gillian Shephard, the then Education and Employment Secretary, argued at the time that it was not credible that four out of five teachers should leave before retirement whereas Nigel de Gruchy, General Secretary of the NASUWT argued that the 'the Government should examine the reasons why so many teachers simply want to escape at the earliest opportunity' (Hackett and Dean 1997).

Faced with facts and figures about practitioners leaving and taking early retirement, we run into the problem discussed earlier of linking such actions to OSI. However it is clear that withdrawing labour like this can be one way of speaking back to reform without making a fuss and it is likely to be an important practitioner response to OSI.

Tokenism

Tokenism can be a powerful form of contestation in situations where more obvious non-compliance with reform would have unacceptably serious consequences for the individual or school. In our EU study Mr Ramsay provides an illustration of tokenism when he talked about a questionnaire he was being asked to circulate to schools:

> I mean, some of the questions you just couldn't answer, it was ridiculous. ... Well, what I did with that was I sent it out to schools without much comment, saying, you know, 'this is what I have to reply by 12th of May, please fill it in as best you can and hand your responses to me'. Nobody replied, and I haven't replied to the DfES. I expect someone will chase me up in a few weeks, and I will say ... 'I haven't heard back from the schools, and you might have actually asked somebody to put in some questions that you could actually ask all schools, you know, it would have been meaningful data for you that you could prepare next year'. But ...

This is a good example of tokenism as a means of contesting policy because the rest of the interview links his lack of enthusiasm for the questionnaire to wider misgivings about the OSI agenda. In many other cases the reasons behind tokenism are not clear. For instance the Head of School Improvement in a large LEA recently mentioned to me that about a third of schools in the LEA were 'not on board' its school improvement programme (which very much reflects OSI). To him this was a problem, but I was left wondering whether these schools did not want to participate because the staff did not agree with the thrust of OSI or because they were already overworked (or both). Perhaps many were like the staff of one of the schools in our EU study, described somewhat scathingly by their headteacher as opposing performative developments in schools because they regarded them as anti-educational:

> You know, the staff were led by a group of very vocal people who were anti-Ofsted. You know, it was all Ofsted's fault, it wasn't anything to do with the school. Ofsted was wrong, Ofsted had the wrong measures. SATs are wrong, you know, they're measuring the wrong things. ... And mixed ability teaching rules, okay? So, within this culture it was politically right to oppose all of those aspects because they were anti-educational, these people were not on board with targeting at all.

The main constraint on tokenism – and fabrication as discussed below – is less likely to be Ofsted inspections which occur only every few years (although twice as often as they used to), as those forms of support/monitoring which are more regular, for instance the work of primary strategy and KS3 consultants. As some schools have been reluctant to get such people in, there are now mechanisms in place to ensure schools provide them with access and cooperation, for instance at secondary level 'intervention grants' require a contract to be drawn up between a school's KS3 strategy manager and its KS3 consultant. At the same time such consultants are typically working with ten secondary schools or 30 primary schools which probably spreads their energies too thinly to really be sure what is going on.

Fabrication

As noted in Chapter 2, Ball (2001) illustrates many forms of fabrication which occur in the 'performing school' by selecting or manipulating statistics and indicators, stage managing events and building the kinds of accounts that schools and individuals construct around themselves. In many ways fabrication is the acceptable face of dishonesty in schools because it is about the necessity, in a culture of performativity and intensification, of putting one's work and achievement in the best possible light through impression management. As in other sectors, heads and teachers fabricate all the time, whether it is for the purposes of marketing schools to parents, meeting performance management targets or doing well in school inspections. For instance in relation to the last, the period between schools hearing they are going to be inspected and the inspection team arriving has been well known for the frenetic, exhausting level of activity generated as schools attempt to shore up areas Ofsted might identify as weaknesses and get a full raft of Ofsted-suitable policies in place.

Because fabrication can work both for and against OSI it is not always about contestation. Where forms of fabrication are sanctioned by OSI, to fabricate can be to comply, for instance, going with the pressure to compete with other schools by talking up one's school in marketing materials, improving a school's position in the league tables by teaching to the test in order to push up KS2 results or using GNVQs to push up five A*–C grades, borrowing school policy documents from government websites and so on. Such activities may simply involve ways to win within the terms of OSI but fabrication can also be an important form of contestation where it provides space for teaching a wider and richer curriculum or for practices which are 'off-message' or marginalized under OSI such as teaching about social inequalities or political processes or teaching a culturally appropriate curriculum. For instance schools might at times teach very explicitly to the test in order to free up curriculum time to address political or social issues which would otherwise be neglected, 'share' Ofsted-suitable policies with other schools in order to spend less time on the development of such policies and so help prevent values-drift towards managerialism and de-emphasize the targeting of extra resources to a marginalized group in their communications with parents where this is likely to be unpopular with a dominant or advantaged group.

Used in this way to contest OSI, fabrication taps into what Sergiovanni (2001) calls 'building in canvas'. That is, like decoys of tanks built in canvas during the war, it allows a do-able option by helping with the issue of legitimacy when schools have to respond to demands and pressures from external audiences which require that schools look the way they are 'supposed to' (Sergiovanni 2001: 10).

Cheating, lying and stealing

Cheating, lying and stealing in ways serious enough to be illegal may not come to mind as contestation practices but nevertheless be regarded by some heads and teachers as legitimate covert responses to OSI policy which is inequitable or anti-educational. For instance a teacher or headteacher who 'adjusts' test results to make a school appear more successful in the league tables, who is dishonest to the LEA in order to keep some resource, or who shifts money between budget headings may genuinely consider themselves doing their best by the community, teacher colleagues or students. For obvious reasons we do not know how common such practices are but those which occasionally come to the attention of the media for serious offences are likely to be just the tip of the iceberg, both in the sense of those who actually get caught and those whose activities are too subtle to clearly break the law.

Heads and teachers doctoring SATs test results (e.g. see Fawcett 2004) has been considered serious enough for the QCA to trial special stickers for pupils to seal their test papers. But there are other forms of SATs cheating pointed up by the media, including pupils allegedly being invited to make changes to their answers after their test (e.g. 'Head resigns after SATs investigation' (2002)) and pupils allegedly getting assistance from teachers during the invigilation of tests (e.g. 'Primary school league tables: school test results scrapped after cheating claims' (2004)). Within such areas, teachers and heads 'cheating' practices can be very subtle and it is uncertain to what extent they engage in practices which would never be reported, for instance advice to a student to 'think about it' (an incorrect answer), giving a little extra time for the test or giving a student's answer the benefit of the doubt when marking.

The 'creative' use of school funding is another type of contestation practice which is probably widespread. Certainly Mr Ramsay in our EU study of Wyeham argued that a key problem with schools bidding for funds direct from central government was that they often didn't use the funding for the purposes intended:

> [If funding came to the LEA] I would be able to get in touch with schools and say you have X amount of places in this activity and if you don't want them that is not a problem, we will give them to

someone else. But it is much more the case that at the moment they have their cake and the less they spend, the more they can steal.

While it can be recognized that illegal forms of contestation such as those above do occur, whether they should be celebrated or emulated is another matter. Certainly where there is sufficient contradiction between what is legally required and what is ethically and educationally good practice, educators may have grounds to act outside the law, with much historical precedent to draw upon. However there is always the risk that, however well-meaning, illegal activities will be uncovered and end up doing a school and its staff, students and community more harm than good.

Control, compliance and contestation

So far my argument in this book has moved gradually from 'unofficial' perspectives on OSI to 'unofficial' responses to it, culminating in discussion of covert practices that can be taken by practitioners when public activity would be counter-productive. Such practices will always be controversial but they are an important option for practitioners when New Labour has been so insistent that it has the answers for schools in England and so demanding of educators that they toe the official line. As Whitty (1998: 7) observed: 'New Labour often seems to demand that we are either with the government 100% or we are against it', while Alexander (2004) sums up the pressure to comply as follows:

> It is clear that in the post-2001 era of 'informed professional judgement' to be 'informed' is to know and acquiesce in what is provided, expected and/or required by government and its agencies – DfES, NLNS, Ofsted, QCA, TTA – no less and, especially, no more. You may be steeped in educational research and/or the accumulated wisdom of 40 years in the classroom, but unless you conform to all this official material your professional judgements will be 'uninformed'. As Adonis says in his Policy Network paper, writing of university faculties and departments of education: 'We have *imposed* a new national curriculum for initial teacher training, setting out the standards and content of training courses, which all providers *must* follow' (Adonis, 2001: 14, Alexander's

italics, Adonis's verbs). Not much room for alternative professional judgement there; and little evidence of government relaxing the iron grip of educational centralization. If you teach or train teachers, on the basis of other kinds of knowledge you are uninformed. For 'informed professional judgement', then, read 'political compliance'. (Alexander 2004: 17)

In such a controlling environment, and constantly reformed, it would be little wonder if teachers, heads and their organizations were to become publically compliant in many areas. Yet as illustrated in this and the previous chapters it is quite another matter to argue that this signals acceptance of OSI in the hearts, minds and local practices of heads and teachers. Awareness-raising is clearly part of the equation and whether or not practitioners accept OSI or contest it in the various ways open to them will partly depend on whether academics who provide school improvement advice become agents of OSI or want to contest it also. This issue is the focus of my final chapter.

6 A strange, sweet noise

> And in that silence Edmund could at last listen to the other noise properly. A strange, sweet, rustling, chattering noise – and yet not so strange for he'd heard it before – if only he could remember where! Then all at once he did remember. It was the sound of running water. (from *The Lion, the Witch and the Wardrobe* by C.S. Lewis)

This final chapter is concerned with the messages heads and teachers get about OSI from academic writers. While it is certainly not the case that all academics are ignoring the problems inherent in OSI (as indicated by the literature used in Chapter 2), heads and teachers draw more often on practitioner-oriented educational management literatures – texts on school change, school improvement, school leadership and the like. In this arena most academics have been underplaying OSI's limitations, thus providing support for it. Indeed the lack of searching critique in the education management arena was the main concern of my last book, co-authored with Rob Willmott, *Education Management in Managerialist Times: Beyond the Textual Apologists* (Thrupp and Willmott 2003). This chapter covers some of the same ground by summarizing that account of the school improvement literature and looking at likely theoretical and political explanations for the problem of 'textual apologism'. But updating the earlier discussion, this chapter also notes some promising recent shifts towards more contextualized school improvement analysis and highlights the work of a 'dissenting' school improvement author (Wrigley 2003). Both of these developments illustrate that, although not common, there are alternative sources of textual inspiration for practitioners in the school improvement area. Wrigley's book *Schools of Hope* also acts as a reminder not to reinvent the wheel when progressive thinking from previous decades can provide many leads.

Educational management in managerialist times

The main contribution of *Education Management in Managerialist Times: Beyond the Textual Apologists* (Thrupp and Willmott 2003) was to illustrate that the education management literature generally fails to adequately reflect or respond to the kind of concerns about OSI noted in Chapter 2 but rather, in subtle or more overt ways, acts to prop it up. To do this we drew both on our own fresh reading of education management texts as well as the arguments of earlier dissenting writers like Angus (1994), Ball (1994), Blackmore (1999) and Grace (2000).

To structure our discussion we referred to four broad categories of texts – primarily problem-solving, overt apologism and subtle apologism and textual dissent. The key point about '*primarily problem-solving*' texts is that you would barely know from them that schooling occurs in the context of post-welfarist education reform and structural inequality as they contain little reference to either. In this sense these texts are 'apolitical' but then avoiding a concern with politics or the social context is itself a highly political position, one which fits easily within a technicist and managerialist approach. Compared to texts which are primarily problem-solving, texts which are examples of *overt apologism* bring post-welfarist education reform into the frame more, but their stance is uncritically supportive and they barely acknowledge the social justice concerns associated with it. For overt apologists the problem is generally how to restructure the school so that it fits with the ideologies and technologies of neo-liberal and managerial reform, it is certainly not how to contest that reform. These texts rarely examine the issue of structural inequality in relation to schooling in any depth, although authors of these kinds of texts would no doubt often argue that they regard post-welfarist education reform working towards social justice as well as effectiveness and efficiency. In contrast, *subtle apologism* involves texts which indicate more concern about the context of post-welfarist education reform and about social inequality – and indeed they may include elements of textual dissent. However, they still provide support to market and managerial education either because their critique is insufficiently critical or because their dissenting element is not emphasized enough within their overall account to provide any serious challenge.

These categories of apologism are extremely broad and not in any sense rigidly bounded or intended to portray perspectives which are fixed or static. Within the same category will be writers with somewhat varying perspectives and writers may often write differently for different audiences or move between perspectives even for the same audience, or just write in equivocal ways which are hard to pin down. Individual outlooks can also change markedly, perhaps as a result of some incident which prompts a rethink or sometimes just a dawning realization that something different needs to be done. All of this means that the categories should be regarded as a useful starting point, a way of getting some initial purchase on the educational management literature – but always needing to be further informed by specific arguments about particular writers.

The same is true of texts which are examples of *textual dissent*. These either challenge the textual apologists directly by critique of textual apologism (for instance Ball 1994; Thrupp 1999), or more indirectly by providing an alternative account (for example Blackmore 1999; Grace 1995) but the key point about these accounts is that one is left in no doubt that the authors are seriously concerned about education management texts which do not challenge post-welfarist education reform and structural inequality.

Turning to the school improvement literature more specifically, the starting point in this area was an earlier review in *Schools Making a Difference: Let's be Realistic!*, in which I illustrated that while school improvement writers vary quite widely in their sensitivity to possible social class and market constraints on low social economic status (SES) schools, most of the work in this area was unclear about either the social limits of reform or the likely impact of market policies in education (see Thrupp 1999, Chapter 10). The same review found that issues of social class were often marginalized because school improvement research tends to concentrate on organizational or instructional concerns and only gives limited weight to the social dimensions of schooling. Improvement literature has tended to favour generalized rather than context-specific discussion. This is seldom made explicit – it is more the case that the literature is vague about what sort of students, classrooms or schools are actually under discussion. Another identified problem was the use of notions of school culture which neglect the culture of students and the community, for instance the idea of schools 'moving', 'cruising', 'strolling', 'struggling' and 'sinking' (Stoll and Fink 1998). What was not discussed was the way these various models of school culture related to middle-class schools and working-class schools, white schools and minority/indigenous schools and so on. School improvement studies were also found to be uncritical in their use of generic school effectiveness findings that take little account of school context. Finally, the *Schools Making a Difference: Let's be Realistic*! review suggested that school improvement writers tended to be subtle apologists, more often not taking sufficient account of the difficulties inherent in post-welfarist reforms than overtly promoting them.

Published four years later, *Education Management in Managerialist Times* (Thrupp and Willmott 2003) noted a growing emphasis on the impact of social and political context in school improvement (e.g. Harris 2001; Maden 2001). Yet we also argued that in most school improvement texts readers were still given an insufficiently critical perspective on reform and were encouraged to go along with policy, rather than contest it. Despite close links to policy, school improvement remains an area with some primarily problem-solving texts (e.g. Horne and Brown 1997; Perez *et al.* 1999; Reyes, Scribner and Scribner 1999; Walsh 1999).There are also a few recent texts which might be regarded as more overtly apologist in the way they actively 'sell' recent official school improvement policy (e.g. Brighouse and Woods 1999). However most school improvement texts exemplify more subtle apologism by indicating concern with the wider social and political context but still offering predominantly decontextualized analyses (e.g. Harris 2002a; Hopkins 2001; Gray 2001).

One of the problems we discussed was a reticence of school improvement writers to be critical about the limits of policy. Gray's

(2001) discussion of 'Special Measures', part of the OSI regime in England, provides a concise example. Gray comments:

> The case of so-called 'failing' schools in England, however, presents a situation where questions about the speed and extent of improvement have become crucial to schools' survival. These schools have typically been given only a two year window to secure a turnaround. (p. 16)

Although one senses that Gray thinks this is problematic, he provides no discussion of the rights or wrongs of the policy. Similarly he goes on to raise questions about the supposed success of Special Measures but only in the most gentle way. Instead of saying that firm evidence for the success of Special Measures just isn't there, particularly given Ofsted's weak inspection methodology and highly politicized stance, he uses phrases such as

> Unfortunately, whilst inspectors have doubtlessly been able to convince themselves that changes have occurred in specific cases, more systematic evidence [on improvement in achievement] across large numbers of schools has yet to be published. (p. 17)

and

> evidence on what it is [about improved 'capacities'] which has actually impressed inspectors is harder to come by. (p. 18)

We argued in *Education Management in Managerialist Times* that there are likely to be several reasons why school improvement writers are not more hard-hitting. One is that some school improvement writers may think they can have more influence if they work with policy-makers rather than criticize policy. This may often be true, at least in the short term, but the way 'working from the inside' comes at the cost of academic freedom and integrity is an uncomfortable issue seldom discussed in school improvement circles. The lack of assertive critique may also partly reflect the problem that 'he who pays the piper, plays the tune'. What Fitz (1999: 315) notes about the education management field is also true of school improvement. The discourse is located

> in a material base in which knowledge has a generally recognized exchange value. In this field, for example, it is not unusual for

relations between field occupants to involve a cash nexus. Indeed ... academics and entrepreneurs are expected and/or required to offer practitioners 'practical' guidance on how to make their institutions more effective and productive. This advice is in turn, taken as evidence of their utility and expertise.

Consequently there is much pressure in the school improvement arena for the accounts of writers to be 'useful' for practitioners and 'relevant' to policy. Research contracts and consultancies from the DfES and NCSL are easier to get for education management projects than more 'independent' research funding from the ESRC (Economic and Social Research Council) but are also more likely to come the way of 'on message' academics: the bias towards textual apologists in the NCSL's consultancies noted in Chapter 4 is a case in point. School improvement writers who go with OSI policy will therefore find it easier to construct the individual fabrications which are so much a part of 'getting ahead' as an academic in managerialist times.1 As Ball (1998: 77) has put it, 'the policy entrepreneurs' interests in terms of identity and career, are bound up directly and immediately ... with the success of their dissemination'.

A further problem we noted is that the theoretical perspectives of school improvement writers are often rather uncritical in any case. What Fitz (1999: 318) has written about education management literature is again also true of the school improvement literature:

> EMS [education management studies] looks like a field without an 'ology', that is, many studies are not intellectually underpinned by explicit social theory. Thus it is difficult to see that 'management' is about relative distributions of power and authority and that there are fundamental questions about who holds legitimate authority (and on what basis), if you haven't read your Lukes, Foucault, Weber, Durkheim, Marx, Talcott Parsons, Bernstein, Bourdieu or Giddens, to name just a few.

Finally we argued in *Education Management in Managerialist Times* that interrelated with the theoretical shortcomings, the empirical limitations of the literature also causes constraints. *School Improvement: What's in it for schools?* (Harris 2002a) points to the need for 'context-specific' improvement approaches

(p. 115). Yet for the most part this book offers a conventionally decontextualized school improvement analysis complete with schools which are 'improving', 'failing' 'trapped' and 'dynamic' (pp. 15–16), seemingly because more contextualized findings were not available.

Differentiated school improvement

Since we wrote *Education Management in Managerialist Times,* an encouraging development in the school improvement area has been the extent to which research and advice has begun to focus on the specific contexts of schools in low socio-economic areas. Alma Harris and colleagues have been continuing to work on breaking out of the 'one size fits all' discourses which have plagued the school improvement literature over the last decade. At the same time Ruth Lupton has been illustrating the need for a differentiated approach to school improvement through detailed case studies of low SES schools.

Much of the research of Harris and colleagues has been a response to the government's concern with Schools Facing Challenging Circumstances (SFCC) (Harris and Chapman 2002; Harris 2002b; Reynolds *et al.* 2001) and at first did not seem very promising. For instance, early research for the NCSL ended up stressing the importance of a number of general findings not far removed from the kinds of 'factors' approach traditionally used in school effectiveness studies: vision and values, distributed leadership, investing in staff development, relationships, and community building (Harris 2002b). The same study also suffered from the problem that the specific contexts of the ten schools involved were not adequately identified: indeed apart from all being DfES categorized as SFCC (which only means that 35 per cent+ of students receive FSM and/or that 25 per cent or less of students get five A*–Cs in GCSE). They were selected 'to ensure the schools represented a wide range of contexts and were geographically spread'.

Nevertheless the recent work of Harris and colleagues in this area is stressing the significance of context-specificity much more

(Harris *et al.* 2003; Harris and Chapman 2004; Harris *et al.* 2005). For instance Harris and Chapman (2004: 429) conclude that:

> As the long term patterning of educational inequality looks set to remain, to rely on standard or standardized approaches to school improvement that combine accountability, pressure and blame to force improved performance would seem unwise. In schools in difficult contexts, this is more likely to exacerbate the problem rather than solve it. Instead the evidence would suggest that more locally owned and developed improvement strategies are needed that appreciate school context, best match prevailing conditions and build the internal capacity for development within the school. If the goal of raising performance in schools in difficulty is to be achieved, school improvement approaches that neglect to address the inherent diversity and variability across and within schools in the same broad category will be destined to fail.

This conclusion chimes with Ruth Lupton's (2004) research which has used detailed case studies to illustrate the impact of multiple dimensions of the context of low SES schools including both pupil characteristics (ethnicity, refugees, SEN) and school and area characteristics (urban/rural, market position compared to surrounding schools, LEA admissions policies, school type and history). Like Harris and colleagues, Lupton stresses that these differences between schools in poor areas lead to more and less favourable contexts for school improvement. Her aim is 'not to imply that area context alone is important but to emphasize that the organizational impacts on schools in different kinds of disadvantaged areas can be significantly different' (p. 22). Lupton also makes the point that it is not always apparent what constitutes good practice in these unusual and challenging circumstances. Her (2004) argument for contextualized school improvement policy involves differentiated provision adapted to the specific needs of each school, a systematic recognition that differences in practice have implications for organizational design, redesign of the delivery of core teaching and learning activities, financial incentives for teachers and job and career re-design.

Harris's and Lupton's research has some differences in emphasis with some issues still to be resolved, for instance the extent to which schools can reasonably build internal 'capacity' in the face of particular kinds and combinations of external constraints. However, it does seem that differentiated school improvement is now firmly on the research agenda. This is an important step forward because it will pose a powerful challenge to OSI by constantly highlighting the need to respond to social and organizational complexity in areas like assessment, target setting, inspection, performance management, staffing and funding. With colleagues at the Institute of Education and the University of Bath, I have been recently working on 'Primary school composition and student progress', a large study of compositional effects in Hampshire primary schools funded by the ESRC.[2] This research will also contribute to a differentiated account of school improvement by exploring school policies and practices that can especially help improve student progress in schools with particular kinds of student intake.

'Schools of Hope'

One of the key problems in thinking about more progressive forms of school improvement is that school improvement academics have not done much to look at alternatives to OSI. Thus the parting shot of *Education Management in Managerialist Times* was that 'What is ultimately most frustrating about today's education management literature is that more energy hasn't gone into thinking about this urgent problem' [i.e. how those who lead and manage schools might contest, rather than support, managerialism] (Thrupp and Willmott 2003: 239.

Given this situation, Terry Wrigley's book *Schools of Hope: A New Agenda for School Improvement* (Wrigley 2003) is another 'strange sweet noise' in the school improvement arena because it casts school improvement as part of a wider political and educational project than most of the literature in the area. The first sections – 'Critiques' and 'Dilemmas' – set the scene with wide-ranging critiques of the conventional school effectiveness and school improvement literatures and OSI. But it is the latter part of the book – 'Learning', 'Communities' and 'Futures' – that really opens up the school improvement agenda by looking critically at 'ability' and 'intelligence', exploring alternative models of curriculum and pedagogy, and raising issues of democracy, community involvement and social justice.

Wrigley's discussion in this part of the book is again very wide-ranging and not particularly joined up. But what is refreshing about this text and the key to its considerable success is that Wrigley is drawing ideas from sources outside the school improvement field, often from progressive educational thinking of previous decades and also from other countries. Put another way, the discussion is not reactive to OSI as so much school improvement literature is, rather Wrigley is willing to go in different directions for more authentic answers to improving schools. Hence although Wrigley (2001) has commented that his questioning of the conventional school improvement agenda has been considered 'virtually heretical', his work does offer a much wider vision of education to inspire heads and teachers than most other school improvement texts as well as many ways forward for the school improvement movement itself.

Concluding thoughts

While school life presents numerous opportunities for savvy practitioners to act progressively without putting their careers on the line, working against the thrust of OSI will never be easy and holds the potential for conflict with local communities, other teachers and senior management, not to mention local education authorities and government agencies such as Ofsted and the DfES. It is therefore crucial to carefully assess the political risk of particular activities and seek supportive alliances within or beyond one's school where possible.

Such collaboration will often be with like-minded people but it is important not to cut off potential allies in unexpected places too. A reminder of this is a joint press release released in 2002 by SHA and the Headmasters' & Headmistresses' Conference (HMC), a professional body for the heads of private schools. The latter were lending their support to a campaign against league tables which they recognized were damaging even though their member schools often top the league tables because of their advantaged intakes and additional resources (SHA press statement 'Heads call for end to school league tables' 15 March 2002). Similarly it is important to reiterate that even those charged with delivering OSI to schools will often be concerned about its limitations even if they feel unable to act on their concerns. Indeed there will be a range of views on OSI within central and local government, with few sharing the level of enthusiasm shown by architects of OSI like Michael Barber (Barber 2000).

In working with others to contest OSI, the way things are done will have a huge influence on what is eventually achieved. Sachs (2003) offers a set of principles for activist teacher professionalism which are applicable to all educators trying to bring about change in education. They include the need for

- Inclusiveness rather than exclusiveness
- Collective and collaborative action
- Effective communication of aims and expectations
- Recognition of the expertise of all parties involved
- Creating an environment of trust and mutual respect
- Ethical practice
- Being responsive and responsible
- Acting with passion
- Experiencing pleasure and having fun. (Sachs 2003: 147–9)

Finally it is important to celebrate – publicly if possible or quietly if need be – any apparent successes in contesting OSI. As long as there is little sign of OSI improving on its own, even minor successes may actually represent very significant achievements in the balance sheet of educational politics and could also pre-empt a slide to policy which is even worse. The truth is that we do not yet have a good picture of the 'unofficial' stances heads and teachers are currently taking or the practices which stem from these. What is certain though is that practitioners committed to contesting OSI will help the present long winter in England's schools eventually pass.

Recommended reading

For those wishing to read more about the themes of this book but unsure where to start, here are ten recommendations from the author for initial further reading:

1. Tomlinson, S. (2005) *Education in a Post-welfare Society* (2nd edn), Abingdon: Open University Press/McGraw-Hill.

Sally Tomlinson's book provides a unique chronological overview of education policy developments in the English education system over the last sixty years and goes into the events and legislation which they have involved in some detail. It also highlights the key social justice concerns and controversies in terms of class, race and ethnicity over the same period. The second edition has been updated to include New Labour's second term from 2001–2005. A 'must-read' for anyone unfamiliar with the English education policy context and a great reference to dip into even for those more familiar with it.

2. Davies, N. (2000) *The School Report*, London: Vintage.

Written by the awarding-winning *Guardian* investigative journalist Nick Davies, this book provides a very readable critique of school level education policy during New Labour's first term. One of the chapters 'Money Matters: A tale of two schools' provides a particularly evocative account of the impact of both social inequality and government policy on the work of schools which cater for the children of the wealthy and the poor. Davies (2000: 47) also stresses that New Labour's attempts to address achievement have been undone by the inequities left in place through retaining the Conservatives' market reforms:

> You can see the strain in the system as David Blunkett's department struggles to put up its tent in the howling gale of Lord Baker's [market] reforms, desperately trying to lash everything together with more and more central command: action plans, school development

plans, LEA education development plans, target setting, benchmarking, naming and shaming, appraisal, baseline assessment, self assessment, national assessment, records of achievement, best value studies, Ofsted inspections, pre-Ofsted inspection, LEA inspections. And still Lord Baker's market wins.

3. Gewirtz, S. (2002) *The Managerial School*, London: Routledge.

Many of the kinds of impacts of OSI in schools discussed in Chapter 2 of this book are raised in Sharon Gewirtz's text which provides a rich, empirically based, account of the effects of managerialism on schools, their leaders, teachers and students. Like Sally Tomlinson's book, it considers New Labour's policies against a background of the Conservatives' policies. An informative critical account which provides a social justice audit of education policy and highlights contradictions within it.

4. Gronn, P. (2003) *The New Work of Educational Leaders*, London: Paul Chapman.

The discussion of designer leadership and the NCSL in Chapter 4 drew on this book by Peter Gronn. The first half of the book, 'The architecture of leadership', is primarily concerned with mapping and critiquing recent trends in educational leadership. It examines 'designer' leadership, 'distributed' patterns of leadership and the 'disengagement' of teachers from school leadership. The second half, 'The ecology of leadership', draws lessons from research on the practice of leadership, including leadership work in committees and teams and the emotions of leadership. It is one of those books best read for its individual chapters but is well worth persevering with because it contains numerous insights into both the actual practices of leadership and the way school leadership is being framed up in managerialist times. Gronn is asking harder questions about leadership and demonstrates more concern with the impact of managerialism on leadership than most other writers in the area.

5. Gray, J. (2001) 'Introduction: building for improvement and sustaining change in schools serving disadvantaged communities', in M. Maden (ed.) (2001) *Success Against the Odds – Five Years On*, London: Routledge Falmer.

Although coy about the impact of national policy on schools, this short chapter by John Gray provides an excellent discussion of the limits and possibilities of school improvement. Among other things, Gray argues that:

> First ... most of the literature simply asserts that 'improvement' has taken place. ... Second, the extent to which improvement is reported to have taken place is heavily dependent on whose perceptions are given greatest weight. ... Third, ... progress in one area may well be at the expense of progress in others. Fourth, there is as yet little agreement about the timescales over which *major* improvements take place. ... Fifth, changes to school management and organization seem easier to secure than changes to classroom practice. ... Sixth, ... most studies to date have been rather short on evidence of *measured* improvements over time. ... Seventh, some researchers have argued that it is more difficult for schools serving disadvantaged areas to make progress on many of the traditional indicators ... [more] evidence on this issue is needed. Finally, there is a shortage of evidence about the extent to which schools manage to sustain improvement. (Gray 2001: 18–19, his emphasis)

Such acknowledgement of the extent to which school improvement is empirically 'up for grabs' is refreshing. A more worthwhile read than most accounts of school improvement.

6. Lupton, R. (2004) Schools in disadvantaged areas: recognizing context and raising performance. CASE paper 76, London: Centre for Analysis of Social Exclusion, London School of Economics and Political Science.

See main text, Chapter 6, for the important contribution Lupton's work is making.

7. Thrupp, M. and Willmott, R. (2003) *Educational Management in Managerialist Times: Beyond the Textual Apologists*, Buckingham: Open University Press.

Provides a critical review of recent educational management literature. As well as school improvement, there are chapters which critically consider the literatures on educational marketing, school development planning and strategic human resource management, school leadership and school change. See Chapter 6 of this book for some discussion of this text.

8. *Rethinking Schools*. The US journal for progressive educators, to be found at www.rethinkingschools.org, and discussed in Chapter 5 of this book.

9. Wrigley, T. (2003) *Schools of Hope: A New Agenda for School Improvement*, Stoke on Trent: Trentham Books.

Chapter 6 of this book describes the important contribution this book makes to the school improvement area.

10. The *TES* (Times Educational Supplement) Archive.

A (free) search tool rather than a particular reference but extremely helpful for anyone trying to keep up with schooling developments in the UK. Simply go to the *TES* website (www.tes.co.uk) and select the *TES* archive. You can then use keywords to bring up *TES* articles related to your interest and can limit your search by section of the *TES* or by date.

Notes

Chapter 1   Introduction

1. For instance in New Zealand there is a similar insistence that quality teaching and management is a more important influence on student achievement than social structures (e.g. Minister of Education 2003: 38). There is also a growing emphasis on what Gronn (2003) calls 'Designer leadership' (see main text, Chapter 4). In other words, the New Zealand Ministry of Education is putting increasing emphasis on a particular model of school leadership and in many ways it is a similarly managerialist and performative model to that being promoted by New Labour in England. It is also possible to see similar policy 'levers' to those in England being increasingly used in New Zealand. These include literacy and numeracy 'strategies', target setting, published school-by-school results, the development of a bidding culture ('honey pot' management) performance management for teachers, increased intervention in failing schools, a web-based portal for school leaders (*LeadSpace*) and new training programmes for existing principals and teachers aspiring to be principals. There is also some more overt evidence of links to England on Ministry of Education websites.

Chapter 2   Always winter and never Christmas

1. Under developments announced in 2004, the SEU was closed and its functions taken over by other parts of the DfES.
2. See Davies (2000).
3. I am grateful to Margaret Brown for this point.
4. There is however continuing debate in England about the extent to which quasi-market policies have added to pre-existing levels of social segregation between schools. See Ball *et al.* (2002: 19) who describe the evidence as 'contradictory and contested', also Thrupp (2001b) and Goldstein and Noden (2003). In New Zealand there has been much more agreement that quasi-markets have polarized schools, see Lauder *et al.* (1999) and Nash and Harker (1998).

5. Reported in the *Guardian*, 26 January 2004.

Chapter 3   Just one piece of Turkish Delight?

1. This section is based on a paper, 'Official School Improvement: Change and Continuity at Ofsted 1997–2004', presented at the 'New Labour Education Policy and Social Justice' Symposium, BERA, Manchester, 15–19 September 2004.

2. Canovan (2002c) reports that in his first address as Chief Inspector Tomlinson reputedly got heartfelt applause when he promised staff two things: that he would not speak on any subject about which he knew nothing, and that everything he said would be based on evidence.

3. An Ofsted adjudicator had been in place from 1998 but was appointed by Ofsted and relatively powerless to affect change (Mansell 2001d).

4. This has also been helped by the availability of Pupil Level Annual School Census (PLASC) data and newly available data from the 2001 census.

5. See Davies (2000) for a good case study of why this does not necessarily follow.

Chapter 4   Even the trees are on her side

1. The section is based on a paper 'The National College for School Leadership: A Critique' presented to the Society for Educational Studies annual seminar on 'School Leadership and Social Justice', London, 4 November 2004.

2. This problem has also been recently underlined by the speakers chosen for one of the NCSL's 'most significant' conferences of 2005. Speakers announced for the 'Seizing Success' conference included:

- David Bell – Ofsted
- Mary Robinson – Executive Director, Ethical Globalization Initiative and former President of Ireland
- Dr John Dunford – Secretary, Secondary Heads Association
- David Hart OBE – General Secretary, National Association of Headteachers

- Professor David Hopkins – Chief Advisor on School Standards at the DfES
- Michael Fullan, Dean of the Institute of Education, University of Toronto
- Professor Brian Caldwell, Dean of Education, University of Melbourne
- Vicki Phillips, Superintendent of Portland Public Schools, Oregon, USA
- Mike Gibbons, Lead Director, The Innovation Unit
- Tony Mackay, Director, Centre for Strategic Thinking, Australia
- Ben Page, Director, MORI Social Research Institute.

There was also to be a keynote speech from a senior government minister.

3. Bastard leadership is so-called because of its similarities to bastard feudalism in the later Middle Ages whereby former feudal relationships retained their surface appearance but had actually become centred on a cash economy. To Wright (2001: 280) school leadership has suffered the same fate of becoming something different while retaining a superficial similarity.

Chapter 5   Best keep down here

1. Others include the Association of Teachers and Lecturers (ATL); the Professional Association of Teachers (PAT), a union whose policy it is never to go on strike; and the Headmasters' & Headmistresses' Conference (HMC), a professional body for the heads of private schools.

Chapter 6   A strange, sweet noise

1. In contrast the policy sociologists who produce many of the critiques of policy raised in Chapter 2 are typically under less pressure than school management and leadership academics to do 'useful' research and teaching. Indeed they can advance their careers through work which provides a trenchant critique of government policy This is not to suggest the work of policy sociologists is

without ethical tensions. Ball (1997: 258) argues that 'critical researchers, apparently safely ensconced in the moral high ground, nonetheless make a livelihood trading in the artefacts of misery and broken dreams of practitioners. None of us remains untainted by the incentives and disciplines of the new moral economy.'

2. ESRC reference: RES-000-23-0784. The local name for this project is HARPS (Hampshire Research with Primary Schools).

References

From newspapers (no author)

'Are your reports bland and useless?' (2003) *Times Educational Supplement*, 7 March.

'Does Ofsted ignore effects of poverty?' (2002) *Times Educational Supplement*, 15 November.

'Fixation with targets "damaging" teacher morale' (2003) *Guardian*, 28 February.

'Head resigns after SATs investigation' (2002) *Times Educational Supplement*, 27 June.

'Inspectors to concentrate on poorly performing councils' (2002) *Times Educational Supplement*, 8 March.

'Keep the chief' (2001) *Times Educational Supplement*, 14 September.

'Ministerial diktat will stifle heads' (2005) *Times Educational Supplement*, 14 January.

'Primaries too focused on targets' (2003) *Guardian*, 5 February.

'Primary school league tables: school test results scrapped after cheating claims' (2004) *Times Educational Supplement*, 2 December.

'Self-evaluation is their future' (2002) *Times Educational Supplement*, 5 April.

'Teachers to quit in droves' (2000) *Times Educational Supplement*, 3 March.

Abrams, F. (2004) 'Shock rise in "failures"', *Times Educational Supplement*, 16 January.

Adonis, A. (2001) *High Challenge, High Support*, London: Policy Network.

Alexander, R. (2004) 'Still no pedagogy? Principle, pragmatism and compliance in primary education', *Cambridge Journal of Education*, 34(1), 7–33.

Angus, L. (1994) 'Sociological analysis and educational management: the social context of the self-managing school', *British Journal of Sociology of Education*, 15(1), 79–91.

Apple, M. W. and Beane, J. A. (eds) (1999) *Democratic Schools: Lessons from the Chalkface*. Buckingham: Open University Press.

Bagley, C., Woods, P. A. and Glatter, R. (2001) 'Implications of school choice policy: interpretation and response by parents of students with special educational needs', *British Education Research Journal*, 27(3), 287–307.

Ball, S. J. (1993) 'What is policy? Texts, trajectories and tool boxes', *Discourse*, 13 (2), 10–17.

Ball, S. J. (1994) *Educational Reform: A Critical and Post-Structural Approach*. Buckingham: Open University Press.

Ball, S. J. (1997) 'Policy sociology and critical social research: a personal review of recent education policy and policy research', *British Educational Research Journal*, 23(3), 257–74.

Ball, S. J. (1998) 'Educational studies, policy entrepreneurship and social theory', in Slee, R., Tomlinson, S. with Weiner, G. (eds) *School Effectiveness for Whom?* London: Falmer.

Ball, S. J. (1999) 'Labour, learning and the economy: A "policy sociology" perspective', *Cambridge Journal of Education*, 29(2), 195–206.

Ball, S. J. (2001) 'Performativities and fabrications in the education economy: towards the performative society', in Gleeson, D. and Husbands, C., (eds) *The Performing School*. London: RoutledgeFalmer.

Ball, S. J. (2003) *Class Strategies and the Education Market*. London: RoutledgeFalmer.

Ball, S. J., Marques-Cardoso, C., Neath, S., Vincent, C. and Thrupp, M. (2004) Workpackage 9 (Interim report to the EU for the project 'Changes in regulation modes and social repro-duction of inequalities'). London: Institute of Education/King's College London.

Ball, S. J., Marques-Cardoso, C., Reay, D., Thrupp, M. and Vincent, C. (2002) *Education policy in England: changing modes of regulation 1945–2001*. (Interim report to the EU for the project 'Changes in regulation modes and social repro-duction of inequalities'). London: Institute of Education/King's College London.

Ball, S. J., Thrupp, M., Vincent, C., Marques-Cardoso, C., Neath, S. and Reay, D. (forthcoming) 'L'Angleterre', in Maroy, C.

(ed.), Ecole, Régulation et Marché, Paris: Presses Universitaires de France.

Bangs, J. (2004) 'Mind your language, Ofsted', *Guardian*, 3 February.

Barber, M. (2000) 'High expectations and standards for all: no matter what', *Times Educational Supplement*, 7 July.

Beckett, F. (2005) 'Not good enough', *EducationGuardian*, 18 January.

Bell, D. (2003a) Access and achievement in urban education: 10 years on. Speech to the Fabian Society, London, 20 November.

Bell, D. (2003b) Reporting for England. Speech to City of York Council Annual Education Conference, 28 February.

Blackmore, J. (1999) *Troubling Women, Feminism, Leadership and Educational Change*. Buckingham: Open University Press.

Blunkett, D. (2000a) NCSL Remit letter 25 September 2000. London.

Blunkett, D. (2000b) Transforming secondary education. Speech to the Social Markets Foundation, London, 15 March.

Bolam, R. (2004) 'Reflections on the NCSL from a historical perspective', *Educational Management, Administration and Leadership*, 32(3), 251–67.

Boothroyd, C., Fitz-Gibbon, C., McNicholas, J., Thompson, M., Stern, E. and Wragg, T. (1997) *A Better System of Inspection?* Hexham: Ofstin.

Bottery, M. (2000) *Education, Policy and Ethics*. London: Continuum.

Bottery, M. and Wright, N. (2000) *Teachers and the State: Towards a Directed Profession*. London: Routledge.

Brighouse, T. and Woods, D. (1999) *How To Improve Your School*. London: Routledge.

Brown, D. (2003) 'Schools plan "is falling short"', *Guardian*, 26 May.

Brown, P. and Lauder, H. (2002) 'Education, class and economic competitiveness', in Scott, A. and Freeman-Moir, J. *Yesterday's Dreams: International and Critical Perspectives on Social Class and Education*: Canterbury: University of Canterbury Press.

Burnham, N. (2002) 'Community shocked as head resigns over report', *Times Educational Supplement*, 19 July.

Bush, T. (2004) 'Editorial: The National College for School Leadership', *Educational Management, Administration and Leadership*, 32(3), 243–9.

Campbell, C., Gold, A. and Lunt, I. (forthcoming) 'An exploration of leadership values in action: conversations with six school leaders', *International Journal of Leadership in Education*.

Canovan, C. (2002a) 'Inspection attitudes show radical change', *Times Educational Supplement*, 5 April.

Canovan, C. (2002b) 'Inspect yourselves, OFSTED tells schools', *Times Educational Supplement*, 5 April.

Canovan, C. (2002c) 'Chasing the inspection demon', *Times Educational Supplement*, 16 April.

Clancy, J. (2002) 'Inspectors talk down authorities', *Times Educational Supplement*, 20 September.

Connell, R. W. (1994) 'Poverty and education', *Harvard Educational Review*, 64(2), 125–49.

Crouch, C., Finegold, D. and Sako, M. (1999) *Are Skills the Answer?* Oxford: Oxford University Press.

Curtis, P. (2003a) 'Raising standards "impossible" in some schools', *Guardian*, 5 February.

Curtis, P. (2003b) 'Labour neglecting inner-city schools', *Guardian*, 20 November.

Curtis, P. (2004a) 'Ofsted criticises primary "superhead" scheme', *Guardian*, 20 August.

Curtis, P. (2004b) 'Autumn figures indicate tougher Ofsted', *Guardian*, 6 February.

Davies, N. (2000) *The School Report*. London: Vintage.

Day, C., Harris, A., Hadfield, M., Tolley, H. and Beresford, J. (2000) *Leading Schools in Times of Change*. Buckingham: Open University Press.

Dean, C. (2000) 'The cost of victory for Summerhill', *Times Educational Supplement*, 31 March.

DfEE (2000) *School Improvement Strategies: the UK approach*. DfEE Publications: Nottingham.

DfEE (2001) *Schools: Building on Success*. London: HMSO.

DfES (2001) *Schools: Achieving Success*. London: HMSO.

DfES (2003) *Excellence and Enjoyment*. London: DfES.

DfES (2004a) *Primary Strategy Learning Networks: groups of schools working together to improve children's learning – an introduction*. London: DfES.

DfES (2004b) *Five Year Strategy for Children and Learners*. London: DfES.

Docking, J. (ed.) (2000) *New Labour's Policies for Schools*. London: David Fulton.

Earley, P. and Evans, J. (2004) 'Making a Difference?', *Educational Management, Administration and Leadership*, 32(3), 325–38.

Earley, P., Evans, J., Collarbone, P., Gold, A. and Halpin, D. (2002) *Establishing the Current State of School Leadership In England*. London: HMSO.

Fawcett, T. (2004) 'Two year ban for test cheat', *Times Educational Supplement*, 24 September.

Fielding, M. (ed.) (2001) *Taking Education Really Seriously: Four Years' Hard Labour*. London: RoutledgeFalmer.

Fitz, J. (1999) 'Reflections on the field of educational management studies', *Educational Management and Administration*, 27(3), 313–21.

Fitz-Gibbon, C. T. and Stephenson, N. J. (1996) Inspecting Her Majesty's Inspectors: should social science and social policy cohere? Paper presented at the European Conference on Educational Research, Seville, Spain.

Furlong, J. *et al.* (2000) *Teacher Education in Transition: Reforming Professionalism*. Buckingham: Open University Press.

Gale, T. and Densmore, K. (2003) *Engaging Teachers: Towards a radical democratic agenda for schooling*. Maidenhead: Open University Press.

Gewirtz, S. (2000) 'Bringing the politics back in: a critical analysis of quality discourses in education', *British Journal of Educational Studies*, 48(4), 352–70.

Gewirtz, S. (2002) *The Managerial School*. London: Routledge.

Gillborn, D. and Youdell, D. (2000) *Rationing Education: Policy, Practice, Reform, and Equity*. Buckingham: Open University Press.

Glatter, R., Woods, P. A. and Bagley, C. (1997) 'Diversity, differentiation and hierarchy: school choice and parental preferences', in Glatter, R., Woods, P. A. and Bagley, C. (eds) *Choice and Diversity in Education: Perspectives and Prospects*. London and New York: Routledge.

Gleeson, D. and Husbands, C. (eds) (2001) *The Performing School*. London: RoutledgeFalmer.

Gold, A., Evans, J., Earley, P., Halpin, D. and Collarbone, P. (2003) 'Principled Principals? Values-driven leadership', *Educational Management and Administration*, 31(2), 127–38.

Goldstein, H. and Noden, P. (2003) 'Modelling social segregation', *Oxford Review of Education*, 29(2), 225–37.

Grace, G. (1995) *School Leadership: Beyond Educational Management*. London and Washington DC: Falmer.

Grace, G. (2000) 'Research and the challenges of contemporary school leadership: the contribution of critical scholarship', *British Journal of Educational Studies*, 48(3), 231–47.

Grace, G. (2002) *Catholic Schools: Mission, Markets and Morality*. London: Routledge.

Gray, J. (2001) 'Introduction: building for improvement and sustaining change in schools serving disadvantaged communities', in Maden, M. (ed.) *Success Against the Odds – Five Years On*. London: RoutledgeFalmer.

Gronn, P. (2003) *The New Work of Educational Leaders*. London: Paul Chapman.

Gunter, H. (2001) *Leaders and Leadership in Education*. London: Paul Chapman.

Hackett, G. and Dean, C. (1997) 'Early retirement clampdown postponed', *Times Educational Supplement*, 21 February.

Hare, D. (2004) 'Arundhati Roy', *Observer Magazine*, 19 December.

Hargreaves, A. and Goodson, I. (1996) 'Teachers' professional lives: aspirations and actualities', in Goodson, I. and Hargreaves, A. (eds) *Teachers' Professional Lives*. London: Falmer Press.

Hargreaves, A. (1998) 'Review of Woods et al. Restructuring schools, reconstructing teachers', *British Journal of Sociology of Education*, 19(4), 420–21.

Harris, A. (2001) 'Contemporary perspectives on school effectiveness and school improvement', in Harris, A. and Bennett, N. (eds) *School Effectiveness and Improvement: Alternative Perspectives*. London: Continuum.

Harris, A. (2002a) *School Improvement: What's in it for schools?* London: RoutledgeFalmer.

Harris, A. (2002b) 'Effective leadership in schools facing challenging contexts', *School Leadership and Management*, 22(1), 15–26.

Harris, A. and Chapman, C. (2002) *Leadership In Schools Facing Challenging Circumstances*. London: National College for School Leadership.

Harris, A. and Chapman, C. (2004) 'Towards differentiated improvement for schools in challenging circumstances', *British Journal of Educational Studies*, 52(4), 417–31.

Harris, A., Clarke, P., James, S., Harris, B. and Gunraj, J. (2005) *Improving Schools in Difficulty*. London: Continuum Press.

Harris, A., Muijs, D., Chapman, C., Stoll, L. and Russ, J. (2003) *Raising Attainment in Former Coalfield Areas*. DfES: Sheffield.

Hatcher, R. (1998) 'Labour, official school improvement and equality', *Journal of Education Policy*, 13(4), 485–99.

Hatcher, R. (2005) 'The distribution of leadership and power in schools', *British Journal of Sociology of Education*, 26(2), 253–67.

Hatcher, R. and Troyna, B. (1994) 'The "Policy Cycle": A Ball by Ball Account', *Journal of Education Policy*, 9(2), 155–70.

Hayes, D. (2004) 'Watchdog launches shake-up in nursery inspections', *Times Educational Supplement*, 13 August.

HayMcBer (2000*) Research into Teacher Effectiveness: A Model of Teacher Effectiveness*. London: DfES.

Hill, A. (2004) 'Ofsted cribbed school report', *Observer*, 28 November.

Hood, C., Scott, C., James, O., Jones, G. and Travers, T. (1999) *Regulation Inside Government: Waste-Watchers, Quality Police, and Sleeze-Busters*. Oxford: Oxford University Press.

Hopkins, D. (2001) *School Improvement for Real*. London: RoutledgeFalmer.

Horne, H. and Brown, S. (1997) *500 Tips for School Improvement*. London: Kogan Page.

Hursh, D. (2005) 'The growth of high-stakes testing in the US: Accountability, markets and the decline in educational equality', *British Educational Research Journal* 31(5).

Iredale, W. (2004) 'E-mails reveal Whitehall battle to gag Ofsted chief', *Sunday Times,* 29 August.

Jeffrey, B. and Woods, P. (1998) *Testing Teachers. The Effect of School Inspections on Primary Teachers.* London: Falmer Press.

Kelly, A. (2001) ' "Softer" OFSTED to focus on the positive', *Times Educational Supplement,* 7 September.

Kelly, R. (2004) *National College for School Leadership Priorities: 2005–6* (remit letter). London: DfES.

Laar, W. (2004) 'Creativity loses again', *Times Educational Supplement,* 30 January.

Lauder, H., Hughes, D., Watson S., Waslander, S., Thrupp, M., Strathdee, R., Simiyu, I., Dupuis, A., McGlinn, J. and Hamlin, J. (1999) *Trading in Futures: Why Markets in Education Don't Work.* Buckingham and Philadelphia: Open University Press.

Lawton, D. (2000) 'Improving or replacing Ofsted'. Background paper presented to the SCSE Annual Conference on Improving or Replacing Ofsted, Institute of Education, 8 November.

Learner, S. (2001a) 'You're going soft on standards, Woodhead tells his successors', *Times Educational Supplement,* 6 July.

Learner, S. (2001b) 'Soft-touch style but tough on standards', *Times Educational Supplement,* 14 September.

Learner, S. (2001c) 'Inspectors highlight specialist failings', *Times Educational Supplement,* 12 October.

Lupton, R. (2004) *Schools in Disadvantaged Areas: Recognising Context and Raising Performance* (CASE paper 76). London: Centre for Analysis of Social Exclusion London School of Economics and Political Science.

Macleod, D. (2004a) ' "Doctors" to help ailing schools in Ofsted shake-up', *Guardian,* 15 June.

Macleod, D. (2004b) 'Ofsted awards itself top marks', *Guardian,* 30 July.

Maden, M. (ed.) (2001) *Success Against the Odds – Five Years On.* London: RoutledgeFalmer.

Mahony, P. Menter, I. and Hextall, I. (2004) 'The emotional impact of performance-related pay on teachers in England', *British Educational Research Journal*, 30(3), 435–56.

Mansell, W. (2000a) 'Flawed Ofsted measure attacked', *Times Educational Supplement*, 14 July.

Mansell, W. (2000b), 'Summerhill accuses inspectors of bias', *Times Educational Supplement*, 24 March.

Mansell, W. (2000c) 'Superheads walk out', *Times Educational Supplement*, 17 March.

Mansell, W. (2001a) 'Tomlinson expected to ease inspection burden', *Times Educational Supplement*, 4 May.

Mansell, W. (2001b) 'Inspection will still focus on failure', *Times Educational Supplement*, 29 June.

Mansell, W. (2001c) 'Staff who quit to get a life', *Times Educational Supplement*, 27 April.

Mansell, W. (2001d) 'Call for real chance to challenge inspectors', *Times Educational Supplement*, 27 April.

Mansell, W. and Hackett, G. (2000) 'Retirement to avoid a Fresh Start', *Times Educational Supplement*, 14 April.

Matthews, P. and Sammons, P. (2004) *Improvement through Inspection: An Evaluation of the Impact of Ofsted's Work*. London: Ofsted

McInerney, P. (2003) 'Moving into dangerous territory? Educational leadership in a devolving education system', *International Journal of Leadership in Education*, 6(1), 57–72.

Menter, I., Muschamp, Y., Nicholls, P. and Ozga, J. (1997) *Work and Identity in the Primary School – a Post-Fordist Analysis*. Buckingham: Open University Press.

Minister of Education (2003) *New Zealand School/Nga Kura o Aotearoa*. Wellington: Minister of Education.

Moore, A., George, R. and Halpin, D. (2002) 'The developing role of the headteacher in English schools', *Educational Management and Administration*, 30(2), 173–88.

Mulford, B. (2004) 'Organizational life cycles and the development of the National College for School Leadership: An Antipodean view', *Educational Management, Administration and Leadership*, 32(3), 309–24.

Nash, R. and Harker, R. (1998) *Making Progress: Adding Value in Secondary Education.* Palmerston North: ERDC Press.

NASUWT (2004) 'NASUWT Briefing: The DfES Five Year Strategy for Children and Learners'. London: NASUWT.

NCSL (2002) 'Final Report'. Nottingham: NCSL.

NCSL (2003) 'Your introduction to NCSL'. Nottingham: NCSL.

Newton, P. (2001) 'National College for School Leadership: an emerging agenda for the leadership development framework', *School Leadership*, (4), 11–14.

Noden, P. (2000) 'Rediscovering the impact of marketisation: dimensions of social segregation in England's secondary schools, 1994–99', *British Journal of Sociology of Education*, 21(3), 371–90.

NUT (2004) *Bringing Down the Barriers.* London: Ofsted.

Ofsted (2003a) *Handbook for Inspecting Nursery and Primary Schools.* London: Ofsted.

Ofsted (2003b) *Annual report of HMCI 2001–2.* London: Ofsted.

Ofsted (2003c) *Inspecting Your School.* London: Ofsted.

Ofsted (2003d) *Leadership and Management: Managing the Workforce.* London: Ofsted.

Ofsted (2004a) *2003 PANDA Report for An Anonymous Secondary School.* London: Ofsted.

Ofsted (2004b) *Annual report of HMCI 2002–3.* London: Ofsted.

OPSR (2003) The Government's Policy on Inspection of Public Services. London: The Prime Minister's Office of Public Service Reform.

Osborn, M. and Broadfoot, P. (1992) 'The impact of current changes in English primary schools on teacher professionalism', *Teachers College Record*, 94(1), 138–51.

Ozga, J. and Walker, J. (1995) 'Women in educational management: theory and practice', in Limerick, B. and Lingard, B. (eds) *Gender and Changing Educational Management.* Sydney: Hodder Headline.

Perez, A., Milstein, M., Wood, C. and Jacquez, D. (1999) *How to Turn a School Around.* Thousand Oaks, CA: Corwin.

Phipps, C. (2004) 'Conscientious objectors', *EducationGuardian,* 30 November, 2–3.

Reay, D. (1998) 'Micro-politics in the 1990s: staff relationships in secondary schooling', *Journal of Educational Policy*, 13(2), 179–86.

Revell, P. (2004) 'Don't look back', *EducationGuardian*, 21 September.

Review Team (2004) *School Leadership: End to End Review of School Leadership Policy and Delivery*. London: DfES and NCSL.

Reyes, P., Scribner, J. D. and Scribner, A. P. (1999) *Lessons From High-Performing Hispanic Schools: Creating Learning Communities*. New York and London: Teachers' College Press.

Reynolds, D., Hopkins, D., Potter, D. and Chapman, C. (2001) *School Improvement for Schools Facing Challenging Circumstances: A Review of Research and Practice*. London: DfES.

Ryan, C. (2004) 'Chief inspector drags watchdog into the spotlight', *Times Educational Supplement*, 13 February.

Sachs, J. (2003) *The Activist Teaching Profession*. Maidenhead: Open University Press.

Sergiovanni, T. J. (2001) *Leadership: What's in it for Schools*. London: RoutledgeFalmer.

SHA (2003) *Towards Intelligent Accountability for Schools*. London: SHA.

SHA (2004) *Intelligent Accountability: One Year On*. London: SHA.

Shaw, I., Newton, D. P., Aitkin, M. and Darnell, R. (2002) 'Do Ofsted inspections of secondary schools make a difference to GCSE results?', *British Educational Research Journal*, 29(1), 63–75.

Shaw, M. (2002a) 'Back in 1992, they had never heard of Woodhead', *Times Educational Supplement*, 15 November.

Shaw, M. (2002b) 'Warning: staffing crisis will get worse', *Times Educational Supplement*, 21 June.

Shaw, M. (2002c) 'Concern at rise of huge inspection firms', *Times Educational Supplement*, 1 November.

Shaw, M. (2002d) ' "Feel free to see the way we work", says inspector', *Times Educational Supplement*, 4 October.

Shaw, M. (2003a) 'Specialists prove less than outstanding', *Times Educational Supplement*, 7 February.

Shaw, M. (2003b) 'Curse of initiatives strikes yet again', *Times Educational Supplement*, 30 May.

Shaw, M. (2003c) 'Ofsted finds little action in city zones', *Times Educational Supplement*, 6 June.

Shaw, M. (2003d) 'Hate targets? So does Ofsted', *Times Educational Supplement*, 28 February.

Shaw, M. (2003e) 'End pay inequality, inspectors urge', *Times Educational Supplement*, 25 July.

Shaw, M. (2003f) 'Lighter inspections to be more rigorous', *Times Educational Supplement*, 30 May.

Shaw, M. (2003g) 'Huge surge in failing schools worries MPs', *Times Educational Supplement*, 7 November.

Shaw, M. and Slater, J. (2003) 'Chief inspector joins chorus against tests', *Times Educational Supplement*, 21 February.

Slater, J. (2003a) 'Private sector fails to deliver', *Times Educational Supplement*, 4 April.

Slater, J. (2003b) 'Leaders not easing teachers' burden', *Times Educational Supplement*, 19 December.

Slater, J. (2003c) 'Ofsted slates skills of staff', *Times Educational Supplement*, 12 December.

Slater, J. (2003d) 'Exodus slows but thousands still quit', *Times Educational Supplement*, 27 June.

Slater, J. (2004a) 'Fiasco of £21 million drive to boost 3Rs', *Times Educational Supplement*, 20 August.

Slater, J. (2004b) 'Failure provides "an opportunity" ', *Times Educational Supplement*, 30 January.

Slater, J. (2004c) ' "Fault may be ours", says Ofsted chief', *Times Educational Supplement*, 7 May.

Slater, J. (2004d) 'Two-day warning of laser inspections', *Times Educational Supplement*, 13 February.

Slater, J. (2004e) 'Heads need to speed read through bumf', *Times Educational Supplement*, 28 May.

Slater, J. and Bushby, R. (2004) 'Inspections cut to the bone', *Times Educational Supplement*, 7 May.

Slater, J. and Shaw, M. (2004) 'Ofsted plans surprise visits', *Times Educational Supplement*, 18 June.

Smithers, R. (2004) 'Number of schools in special measures rises', *Guardian*, 7 February.

Smyth, J. (1989) *Critical Perspectives on Educational Leadership*. London: Falmer.

Smyth, J. (ed.) (1993) *A Socially Critical View of the Self-Managing School*. London and Washington DC: Falmer.

Southworth, G. (2004) 'A response from the National College for School Leadership', *Educational Management, Administration and Leadership*, 32 (3), 339–54.

Stark, M. (1998) 'No slow fixes either', in Stoll, L. and Myers, K. (eds) *No Quick Fixes: Perspectives on Schools in Difficulty*. London and Washington DC: Falmer Press.

Stewart, W., Smith, N. and Slater, J. (2004) 'Ofsted chief's call for clarity', *Times Educational Supplement*, 12 March.

Stoll, L. and Fink, D. (1998) 'The cruising school: the unidentified ineffective school', in Stoll, L. and Myers, K. (eds) *No Quick Fixes: Perspectives on Schools in Difficulty*. London and Washington DC: Falmer Press.

Taylor, M. (2005) 'Kelly jeered at heads' conference', *Guardian*, 5 March.

Thornton, K. (2002a) 'Headships go out of fashion', *Times Educational Supplement*, 17 May.

Thornton, K. (2002b) 'Teachers retire as early as possible', *Times Educational Supplement*, 6 December.

Thrupp, M. (1998) 'Exploring the politics of blame: school inspection and its contestation in New Zealand and England', *Comparative Education*, 34(2), 195–209.

Thrupp, M. (1999) *Schools Making a Difference: Let's be Realistic!* Buckingham and Philadelphia: Open University Press.

Thrupp, M. (2001a) 'New Labour and "failing" schools: policies, claims and evidence'. Paper presented to the SCSE Annual Conference on 'Education, Education, Education: A

Commitment Renewed'. London: Institute of Education, 15 November, 2001.

Thrupp, M. (2001b) 'School quasi-markets in England and Wales: Best understood as a class strategy?' Paper presented to the BERA Annual Conference, Leeds, 13–15 August.

Thrupp, M. (2004) 'Conceptualising educational leadership for social justice', *New Zealand Journal of Educational Administration and Leadership*, 19, 21–9.

Thrupp, M. and Willmott, R. (2003) *Educational Management in Managerialist Times: Beyond the Textual Apologists.* Buckingham: Open University Press.

Thrupp, M., Ball, S. J., Neath, J. S., Vincent, C. and Reay, D. (2003) *Intermediary regulation in Wyeham, England* (Interim report to the EU for the project 'Changes in regulation modes and social reproduction of inequalities'). London: King's College London/Institute of Education: London.

Thrupp, M., Ball, S. J., Vincent, C., Marques-Cardoso, C., Neath, S. and Reay, D. (2004) 'Additive and hyper-regulation of schooling in England: The case of Wyeham', *Recherches Sociologiques*, XXXV(2), 65–81.

Tomlinson, S. (2005) *Education in a Post-welfare Society* (2nd edn). Abingdon: Open University Press/McGraw-Hill.

Tymms, P. (2004) 'Are standards rising in English primary schools?' *British Educational Research Journal*, 30(4), 477–94.

Walker, A. and Dimmock C. (2004) 'The International role of the NCSL: tourist, colporteur or confrere?', *Educational Management, Administration and Leadership*, 32(3), 269–87.

Wallace, W. (2001a) 'Death of a school', *Times Educational Supplement*, 16 February.

Wallace, W. (2001b) 'Is that Better?', *Times Educational Supplement*, 2 February.

Walsh, M. (1999) *Building a Successful School*. London: Kogan Page.

Ward, H. (2001) 'Staff shortage hits primary standards', *Times Educational Supplement*, 7 December.

Ward, H. (2002) 'Primary reading "not good enough"', *Times Educational Supplement*, 29 November.

Ward, H. (2004) 'Inspectors to look before they judge', *Times Educational Supplement*, 13 August.

Weindling, D. (2004) 'Funding for research on school leadership'. Paper available on NCSL website.

White, P. (2002) 'Band of eight set to inspect', *Times Educational Supplement*, 25 October.

Whitty, G. (1998) 'New Labour, education and disadvantage', *Education and Social Justice*, 1(1), 2–8.

Wiliam D. (2001) *Level best? Levels of attainment in national curriculum assessment*. London: The Association of Teachers and Lecturers.

Wolf, A. (2002) *Does Education Matter? Myths about Education and Economic Growth*. London: Penguin.

Woods, P. (1995) *Creative Teachers in Primary Schools: Strategies and Adaptations*. Buckingham: Open University Press.

Woods, P., Jeffrey, B., Troman, G. and Boyle, M. (1997) *Restructuring Schools, Reconstructing Teachers*. Buckingham: Open University Press.

Woodward, W. (2001) 'An inspector calls', *Guardian*, 28 August.

Wragg, E. (2004) 'A hopalong travesty', *Times Educational Supplement*, 25 June.

Wright, N. (2001) 'Leadership, "Bastard" Leadership and Managerialism: Confronting Twin Paradoxes in the Blair Education Project', *Educational Management and Administration*, 29(3), 275–90.

Wright, N. (2003) 'Principled "Bastard" Leadership?', *Educational Management and Administration*, 3(2), 139–43.

Wrigley, T. (2001) 'Editorial: what is the tune and who is the piper?', *Improving Schools*, 4(3), 1–2.

Wrigley, T. (2003) *Schools of Hope: A New Agenda for School Improvement*. Stoke on Trent: Trentham Books.

Index

A
'A-to-C economy' 21
Abraham, Jim 95–6
Activist Teaching Profession, The (Sachs) 5
Alexander, R. 31–2, 102–3
Angus, L. 106
Apple, M. W. 7
ascriptive leadership 54
Association of Teachers and Lectures
    (ATL) 123n.1

B
Bagley, C. 23
Ball, S. J. 10, 19, 21, 99, 106–7, 110,
    121n.4
Bangs, J. 45
Barber, Michael 10, 115
'bastard leadership' 70, 123n.3
Beacon Schools 9, 12, 19, 71
Beckett F. 24
Bell, David 35–42, 44, 46, 48
Birmingham Catholic Secondary
    Partnership 92
Blackmore, J. 106, 107
Blunkett, David 34, 35, 51, 95, 96–7
Boothroyd, C. 16
Bottery, M. 49, 76, 77–8
Bringing Down the Barriers (NUT) 82–3
British Educational Research Association
    (BERA) 88
Broadfoot, P. 4, 6, 75
Brown, P. 17, 18
'building in canvas' 100
Bush, Tony 52, 53

C
Campaign for State Education (CASE) 88
Canovan, C. 33, 36

Capita Group Plc 41
*Changes in Regulation Modes/A European
    Comparison* (Ball) 11
Chapman, C. 112
charter schools 20
citizenship 27
City Academies 9
Communities Empowerment Network
    (CEN) 88–9
Conservative policy 11, 18, 33, 34, 82, 97
credentialist leadership 54
Crouch, C. 18
curriculum prescription 20–1, 46–7
Curtis, P. 42

D
Davies, Nick 117–18, 122n.5
Day, C. 67–9, 78
De Aston School 92–3
de Gruchy, Nigel 97
Densmore, K. 5, 7, 76–7
Department for Education and Skills
    (DfES)
    and accountability 12–13
    evaluation reports of initiatives 11
    Five Year Strategy response 84
    legal challenge 95
    and NCSL 52, 56, 58–60, 64–6
    and OSI 114
    Primary Strategy Networks 92
    and reform refusal 93
    research contracts 110
    and school improvement 111
    Standards and Effectiveness Unit 10
designer leadership 54–6
Dimmock, C. 53
diversity 19, 20, 22, 49
Dunford, Dr John 86–7

E
Earley, P. 54, 69–70, 78
'Eatwell, Mr' 14
Economic and Social Research Council
    (ESRC) 110, 113, 124n.2
Education Action Zones (EAZ's) 10
*Education Management in Managerialist
    Times* (Thrupp/Wilmott) 4, 105–7,
    109, 110, 111, 113
Education in a Post-Welfare Society
    (Tomlinson) 117
*Educational Management, Administration,
    & Leadership* (journal) 52
'educational triage' 24
Effective Headteachers (research project)
    67
Excellence in Cities (EiC) 9, 10, 12
Excellence and Enjoyment (DfES) 29, 31,
    46

F
fabrication 99–100
Finegold, D. 18
Fink, Dean 91
Fitz, J. 109–10
Fitz-Gibbon, Carol 16, 37
*Five Year Strategy for Children and
    Learners* (DfES) 49, 66, 82, 84, 87
'flexible professionalism' 76
Form S4 (OFSTED) 43, 45
free school meals (FSMs) 39
'Fresh Start' initiative 96

G
Gale, T. 5, 7, 76–7
George, R. 71, 72
Gewirtz, S. 22, 23, 25, 71, 118
Gillborn, D. 21, 24, 25
Glatter, R. 22, 23
Gold, Anne 69–71, 78
Grace, Gerald 64, 71, 92, 106, 107
Gray, John 108–9
Gronn, P. 54–6, 118

H
Halpin, D. 71, 72
Hampshire Research with Primary Schools
    (HARP) 113, 124

Hargreaves, A. 75–6
Harris, Alma 110–13
Hatcher, R. 1, 9, 32, 49, 66–9, 77–8
Headmasters' and Headmistresses'
    Conference (HMC) 114–15, 123n.1
Headteacher Induction Programme (HIP)
    55
Headteacher Leadership & Management
    Programme (HEADLAMP) 55
Her Majesty's Chief Inspector of Schools
    (HMCI) 33, 34, 38, 83, 122n.2
Hextall, I. 23
high SES schools 19, 22
Hopkins, David 10, 121
Hursh, D. 7

I
Improving Schools (journal) 94
Institute of Race Relations (IRR) 88
intervention grants 99

J
'Jill' (teacher) 17

K
Kelly, Ruth 66, 88
Key Reads 63
Key Stage testing 15–16, 25, 31–2, 83, 86,
    100
Knowledge pool 60–4
KPMG International 60
KS3 consultants 99

L
Laar, W. 46–7
Lancaster University Management School 63
'laser' inspections (OFSTED) 36–7, 42,
    44, 45
Lauder, H. 17, 18
Lawton, D. 34
Leadbeater, Charles 91
Leadership Network 91
Leadership Programme for Serving
    Headteachers (LPSH) 55
*Leadership in Schools Facing Challenging
    Circumstances* (Harris/Chapman) 111
Leading Schools in Times of Change (Day
    and ors) 67, 68–9

league tables 114–15
Learning Gateway 56, 57
Learning and teaching in the Primary Years (DfES) 30
legal challenge (DfES) 95
'lighter touch' inspections (OFSTED) 42, 45
low SES schools 19
Lupton, Ruth 40, 111, 112–13

M
McBer, Hay 62–3
McInerney, P. 71–2
Macleod, D. 42
Mahoney, P. 23
Managerial School, The (Gerwitz) 118
managerialism 77
Mansell, W. 97
Matthews, P. 37, 38
Menter, I. 23, 78
Miliband, David 41, 91
Models of Excellence for School Leaders (McBer) 62–3
Moore, A. 71, 72
Moorlands Primary School 97
Morris, Estelle 34, 35, 36
'Mr Weller' 73–4
Mulford, B. 53–4

N
National Association of Headteachers (NAHT) 87, 88
National Association of Schoolmasters/ Women Teachers (NASUWT) 83–5, 88, 97
National College for School Leadership (NCSL) 3, 9, 24, 51–78, 91, 110–11, 122n.2
National Curriculum 4, 31, 83
National Numeracy Strategy 14
National Primary Education Alliance (NPEA) 89
National Primary Headteachers Association (NphA) 89
National Professional Qualification for Headteachers (NPQH) 53
National Standards for Headteachers 56
National Union of Teachers (NUT) 45, 82–5, 88

Neal, Tony 92–3
Neill, A. S. 95
New Labour
  and choice 19
  and education policies 1
  and the Knowledge Pool 60–1
  and the NCSL 64, 66
  and Ofsted 9, 16, 20, 33–49
  and OSI 6, 9–10, 75, 102
  and SATs testing 32
  and the workforce 17
New Public Management 54–5
New Work of Educational Leaders, The (Gronn) 54, 118
No Child Left Behind Act 2001 (USA) 7

O
Office for Standards in Education (Ofsted)
  and fabrication 100
  Form S4 43, 45
  'laser' inspections 36–7, 42, 44, 45
  and legal challenges 94–5
  and managerialism 24
  and NAHT policy 87
  and NASUWT policy 85
  and NCSL 53, 60, 66, 70
  and New Labour policy 9, 16, 20, 33–49
  and NPhA policy 89
  and NUT policy 83
  and OSI 3, 5, 75, 81, 114
  and Primary Strategy 32
  and reforms 93
  and Special Measures 109
  teaching and assessment values 21
  and tokenism 99
  work of 29
Osborn, M. 4, 6, 75
overt apologism 106–7

P
pay 32, 84
  performance related (PRP) 23, 24, 81, 87
Performance and Assessment Reports (PANDA) 39, 122n.4
performativity 43–6
Personal Social and Health Education (PSHE) 26

polarization 19–20
'practical professionalism' 76
'primarily problem solving' 106
Primary School Composition (research
    project) 113
Primary Strategy 2, 29–32, 43, 48–9, 60
    Learning Networks 30, 92
'primary superhead scheme' 42
'Principled principals' study 69–71
Professional Association of Teachers (PAT)
    123n.1
proportionality 42, 43–4, 45
Pupil Level Annual School Census (PLASC)
    122n.4

Q
quasi-market policy 19–20, 23, 26

R
'Ramsay, Mr' 11–14, 98, 101–2
Reay, D. 22, 23
research contracts 110
*Restructuring Schools, Reconstructing
    Teachers* (Woods and ors) 75–6
Rethinking Schools (journal) 90
Rethinking Schools organization 89–91
retirement, early 98–9
Reynolds, Professor David 91
Roy, Arundhati 5

S
Sachs, J. 5, 7, 115
Sako, M. 18
Sammons, P. 37, 38
SATs testing 5, 31, 32, 47, 81, 87, 89, 101
School of Hope (Wrigley) 4, 105, 113–14,
    119
*School Improvement; What's in it for
    Schools?* (Harris) 110–11
*School Leadership: Beyond Education
    Management* (Grace) 64
School Report, The (Davies) 117–18
School Standards and Framework Act
    1998 33–4
Schools Facing Challenging Circumstances
    (SFCC) 111
Schools Making a Difference (Thrupp)
    107, 108

Secondary Heads Association (SHA) 38,
    85–7, 88, 114–15
self-evaluation 44–5
SEN pupils 23
Sergiovanni, T. J. 100
SES schools 19, 22, 39, 107, 111, 112
Shaw, M. 35, 36, 37, 45
Shephard, Gillian 97
'Simmons, Mr' 14–15
sink schools 20
Slater, J. 36, 37, 48
special measures schools 42, 45–6, 109
Specialist Schools 9, 19, 20
Standards and Effectiveness Unit (SEU) 10,
    121n.1
Stephenson, N. J. 16
'subcontractors' 67, 68
subtle apologism 106–7
'subversives' 67
Summerhill School 95

T
talk2learn 56, 57
Teachers Pay and Conditions Act (1987)
    82
teaching and assessment values 21
'textual apologism' 4, 6, 105–7
Thornton, K. 25, 97
Times Educational Supplement (TES) 33,
    35, 83, 94, 95–6, 97
tokenism 98–9
Tomlinson, Mike 34, 36, 43, 48, 122n.2
Tomlinson, Sally 117
'trained incapacity' 17
transformational leadership 53
Tymms, P. 16

U
University of Manchester 63

W
Walker, A. 53
Ward, Martin 38, 48
websites
    www.bera.ac.uk (BERA) 88
    www.casenet.org.uk (CASE) 88
    www.compowernet.org (CEN) 89
    www.irr.org.uk (IRR) 88

www.naht.org.uk (NAHT) 87
www.ncsl.org.uk (NCSL) 57–64, 91
www.primaryheads.org.uk (NphA) 89
www.rethinked.org.uk 91
www.rethinkingschools.org (RS) 89
www.sha.org.uk (SHA) 85
www.teachers.org.uk (NUT) 82
www.teachersunion.org.uk (NASUWT) 83
West, Mel 63
What Leaders Read (reviews) 63
Whitty, G. 102

Wiliam, D. 15
Willmott, Rob 4, 93, 105–6, 108, 113
Wolf, A. 17–18
Woodhead, Chris 33, 34, 38, 39–40, 48
Woods, P. A. 4, 6, 23, 75–6
Wragg, E. 45, 48
Wright, N. 49, 67, 69–70, 76–8, 123n.3
Wrigley, T. 4, 113–14, 119
'writer-activist' 5

Y
Youdell, D. 21, 24, 25